WAR POEMS

ACKNOWLEDGEMENTS:

The publisher would like to thank the following people and organisations for permission to reproduce copyright material:

Carcanet Press for permission to reproduce *To His Love, First Time In* and *The Silent One*, by Ivor Gurney.

AP Watt Ltd, on behalf of Gráinne Yeats, for permission to reproduce *An Irish Airman Foresees His Death*, by W. B. Yeats.

The Barbara Levy Literary Agency for permission to reproduce *The General, 'Blighters', Reconciliation* and *Glory of Women*, by Siegfried Sassoon.

The Society of Authors as the Literary Representative of the Estate of Laurence Binyon for permission to reproduce *For the Fallen*, by Laurence Binyon.

David Higham Associates on behalf of Dylan Thomas and J M Dent for permission to reproduce *A Refusal to Mourn the Death, by Fire, of a Child in London*, by Dylan Thomas.

Faber and Faber Publishing on behalf of J.C. Hall for permission to reproduce *Actors Waiting in the Wings of Europe, Aristocrats, Desert Flowers, How to Kill, Simplify Me When I Am Dead,* and *Vergissmeinnicht,* from *Complete Poems,* by Keith Douglas.

David Higham Associates on behalf of Shepheard Walwyn and John Pudney for permission to reproduce *For Johnny, Combat Report* and *Western Desert*, by John Pudney.

David Roberts at www.warpoetry.co.uk and Curtis D. Bennett, for permission to reproduce *Vietnamese Morning* and *America – 'My Country 'tis of Thee',* by Curtis D. Bennett.

FRONT COVER IMAGE:

Dampierre, July 1916 (oil on canvas) by François Flameng / Musée de l'Armée, Paris. Supplied courtesy of Getty Images.

WAR POEMS

EDITED BY VIVIAN HEAD

Abbeydale Press

ISBN 978-1-86147-279-3

1 3 5 7 9 10 8 6 4 2

Published by Abbeydale Press
an imprint of Bookmart Ltd
Registered number 2372865
Trading as Bookmart Ltd
Blaby Road, Wigston, Leicester
LE18 4SE, England

Produced by Omnipress Limited, UK
Cover design by Omnipress Limited, UK

Printed in the UAE

VIVIAN HEAD has written on a wide range of topics, but her real love is literature in all its forms. In this
book she has not only chosen some of her favourite war poems, but she has also delved into the background
behind each conflict. By reading these heart-wrenching poems, the editor hopes it will bring home exactly
what was destroyed on the battlefields.

Contents

Introduction

The traumatic experience of war can never be forgotten, but the way people remember it will always differ. The memories may be those of a soldier who took part in the actual bitter conflicts, or the worker who had to toil long hours for the war effort. Perhaps the memories are happier ones from the people who were evacuated away from the cities to the country, or the landgirls who had to turn to man's work.

Perhaps no one captures the emotions of war better than the poet, who for his or her own personal reason, may have bitter sweet memories.

Rudyard Kipling was extremely patriotic and his poetry was predominantly about those who had died fighting for their country. He used his influence to get his son Jack a commission in the Irish Guards, with tragic consequences. Jack was killed in his first military engagement, at the young age of 18, in the Battle of Loos in September 1915. In an epitaph entitled *My Son* he wrote:

My son was killed while laughing at some jest. I would I knew
What it was, and it might serve me in a time when jests are few.

Many poets throughout the years have captured the emotions of war through their verse. Rudyard Kipling wrote, for example, about the Boer War in his poem *Ubique*:

Ubique means the warnin' grunt the perished linesman knows,
When o'er 'is strung an' sufferin' front the shrapnel sprays 'is foes,
An' as their firin' dies away the 'usky whisper runs,
From lips that 'aven't drunk all day: 'The Guns! Thank Gawd, the Guns!'

After his tragic loss, we see Kipling's emotions turn to bitterness in poems such as *Destroyers in Collision*. Many people were not happy about his bitter memories of war, but as they heard more and more gruelling stories of twisted and torn bodies lying on the battlefields, they came to understand his sentiments.

W. B. Yeats, on the other hand, when asked to write about his feeling towards war simply said:

I think it better that in times like these
A poet's mouth should be silent.

Having said that he went on to write the magnificent *An Irish Airman Forsees His Death*.

I know that I shall meet my fate
Somewhere among the clouds above;
Those that I fight I do not hate,
Those that I guard I do not love.

The poet Rupert Brooke participated in the evacuation of Antwerp in October 1914 and in 1915 was en route with his battalion to take part in the Dardenelles campaign. He became weak from sunstroke and then contracted blood poisoning from a mosquito bite on his lip. Just two days before the landings at Gallipoli, he passed away and was buried on the Island of Skyros. His poems included *Peace, Safety, The Dead* and *The Soldier*.

If I should die, think only this of me:
That there's some corner of a foreign field
That is forever England. There shall be
In that rich earth a richer dust concealed.

Another poet who took part in active service was Wilfred Owen. He suffered from shellshock in 1917, but returned to the front to fight the following year. He won the Military Cross for gallantry, but was killed leading his men on 4 October 1918. His poems were collected and published after the war by Siegfried Sassoon. His poem called *Anthem for Doomed Youth* recalled:

No mockeries now for them; no prayers nor bells;
Nor any voice of mourning save the choirs,
The shrill, demented choirs of wailing shells;
And bugles calling for them from sad shires.

Whether they saw active service or not, many poets have felt compelled to write about the devastation and the futile loss of lives associated with war. This book covers all the major conflicts and war poets and also gives a brief outline of their lives.

About the
Poets

LAURENCE BINYON (1869–1943)

Laurence Binyon was educated at St Paul's School and Trinity College, Oxford. As well as being a poet, Binyon was famous for being a painter and was an authority on English watercolours. He became a professor of poetry at Harvard University in the USA and in 1940 he became Byron professor of English Literature at the University of Athens. One of his most famous poems is *For the Fallen* written in 1914, in which he wrote the immortal words 'They shall not grow old'.

RUPERT (CHAWNER) BROOKE (1887–1915)

Rupert Brooke was a promising English poet who died young in World War I. He was born in Warwickshire and even as a young child he immersed himself in English poetry. Possibly his best known work is *The Soldier* in which, like many other war poets, Brooke glorified war. As the horrors of war became a reality, his poetry lost favour. His courage and chivalry as a fighter became his literary burden and today he is better remembered for his lighter verses and the *Tahiti* poems.

GILBERT KEITH CHESTERTON (1874–1936)

Born in London, Chesterton went on to study at Slade Art School. However, he lost interest in the subject and started writing articles for newspapers and journals such as *The Daily News, The Speaker, The Bookman* and the *Illustrated London News*. The first two books that Chesterton had published were collections of his poetry, *The Wild Knight* in 1900 and *Greybeards at Play* in 1900. These were followed by several biographies and his most popular novel, *The Innocence of Father Brown* in 1911. When the first rumbles of World War I were heard, Chesterton was recruited as head of Britain's War Propaganda Bureau. His work including the writing of two pamphlets *The Barbarism in Berlin* in 1915 and *The Crimes of England* in 1915. In 1922 Chesterton converted to a Roman Catholic, which influenced much of later works. His *Collected Poems* appeared in 1933 just three years before his death.

KEITH DOUGLAS (1920–1944)

Keith Douglas was born in Kent and educated at Oxford University with the help of poet Edward Blunden. He is probably the most well known of the World War II poets and began publishing his work at the age of 16. He enlisted in the British Army at the onset of the war but was sadly killed in Normandy. His poems are at times chilling and often lacked sentiment, portraying a rather obsessive view of death. His work only really received acclaim when an admirer of his edited a volume of his poems in 1964.

EBENEZER ELLIOTT (1781–1849)

Ebenezer Elliott liked to think of himself as 'the poet for the poor', and became a household name in the Sheffield area. Initially he was the owner of an iron foundry, but after a bad spell faced bankruptcy. Elliott's sympathies were with the working man as he knew what it was like to be impoverished and on the edge of starvation. He was unusual for his time, as a working class man, who had an interest in both poetry and politics. Believing that the Corn Laws had been responsible for his downfall, he went on to campaign against them. He had dabbled in poetry since he was 16 years old, and his *Corn Law Rhymes*, published in the 1830s, brought him national fame. These rhymes attacked the landowners and the government; they were aggressive and sarcastic, and drew attention to the atrocious conditions endured by the working classes. Needless to say not everyone appreciated Elliott's work and its content, and he was seen as a revolutionary by many people. Though not best known for his war poems, Elliott did write a poem entitled *The Soldier* and *War* in 1810, which at the time received little acclaim.

FRANCIS MILES FINCH (1827–1907)

Francis Finch was born at Ithaca, New York and was later educated at Yale. He was the Yale class poet for his graduating class in 1849 and editor of the *Yale Magazine*. Finch returned to Ithaca after the death of his wife Eliza Brooke in 1853 and studied law, being admitted to the bar a year later. He was appointed to the board of trustees at Cornell's College of Law where he gave lectures and read out poetry. His own poetry, however, was only published after his death in 1907.

IVOR GURNEY (1890–1937)

Ivor Gurney was born in Gloucester and educated at King's School and the Royal College of Music. Before the onset of World War I, Gurney had started writing poetry and music. Gurney fought for his country but was wounded and suffered the effects of gas, and he was forced to return to Britain. During his convalescence he was diagnosed as a paranoid schizophrenic and had to be committed to a mental hospital. From the confines of the hospital, Gurney continued to write poetry, believing in his mind that he was still taking part in the war. He died of tuberculosis in 1937.

THOMAS HARDY (1840–1928)

Thomas Hardy was born in Dorset, the son of a master stonemason. From his father he learned to love music and the delights of the countryside. Hardy started to write poetry when he moved to London, but his early verses were rejected. Ill health forced him to return to Dorset. In 1870 he met his future wife Emma Gifford, who encouraged him in his writing. His first major success came in 1874 with the serialisation of *Far From the Madding Crowd*, printed in the *Cornhill Magazine*. This was followed by other popular novels such as *Tess of the D'Urbevilles* (1891) and *Jude the Obscure* (1896), but disappointed by the reviews he received for his books, Hardy decided to concentrate on poetry. The remainder of his life was spent writing poetry and when his beloved wife died in 1912, his immense sense of loss led to some of his most powerful verses.

THOMAS ERNEST HULME (1883–1917)

Hulme's interest in poetry was short-lived and he never wrote any large number. In fact the *Complete Poetical Works of T. E. Hulme* published in 1912, only contained five of his poems. However limited in number, Hulme's poems still managed to have an enormous influence. Hulme was a member of the Second Poets' Club which also included Ezra Pound and F. S. Flint. He was also one of the first critics to write about sculpture and modern paintings. He volunteered as an artilleryman in 1914, and served with the Royal Marine Artillery in France and Belgium. He wrote articles for *The New Age* and also wrote a poem entitled 'Trenches: St Eloi' about his experiences during wartime. He was killed by a shell at Oostduinkerke in West Flanders in 1917.

JOHN JARMAIN (?–1944)

Like many of the World War I poets, Jarmain did not survive the war which formed the subject of his poetry. He had a single collection of his poems published posthumously in 1945, but despite being relatively unknown he is certainly worthy of appearing among the better known poets. Little is known about his early life, but he served as an officer with the 51st Highland Division anti-tank unit. He served in the Western Desert, but was eventually killed by a German mortar bomb while on a reconnaisance mission in Normandy. His poems, though few in number, exemplify the courage of those who fought and died while fighting for their country.

RUDYARD KIPLING (1865–1936)

Rudyard Kipling was born in Bombay, India, but was educated in England at the United Services College, Westward Ho, in Bideford, Devon. After his education he returned to India where he worked for a while for the Anglo-Indian newspapers. He became well known for his short stories and, a prolific writer, his fame soon spread. He became the poet of the British Empire and was the recipient of many honorary degrees and awards. In 1926, Kipling received the Gold Medal of the Royal Society of Literature, which had only been awarded to three people before — Scott, Meredith and Hardy. His book, *The Jungle Book*, written in 1894, became a children's classic all over the world. Many of his poems were affectionately drawn portraits of the common soldier, including his *Barrack Room Ballads*, written in 1892.

ALUN LEWIS (1915–1944)

Alun Lewis was born in Wales and from a young age showed a great love of literature and in particular poetry. Lewis greatly admired the work of Edward Thomas, and by 1940 had proved himself as a poet with his first publication, *Raiders Dawn and Other Poems*. Despite being a pacifist, Lewis enlisted in the Royal Engineers in 1940. In early 1944 he was called to go to the Burmese front where his regiment occupied a defensive position. On 5 March 1944 he was the victim of a mysterious accident. At about 5.30 a.m. Lewis had shaved and was on his way to the latrine, carrying a loaded revolver, as military orders demanded. What happenen next is still a mystery. It was reported that in his hurry to get to the latrine, Lewis fell and accidentally shot himself in the head. Lewis's second books of poems, *Ha! Ha! Among the Trumpets* was published posthumously in August 1945.

❧❦❧

HENRY WADSWORTH LONGFELLOW (1807–1882)

Henry Wadsworth Longfellow was the most popular American poet of the 19th century. His works ranged from sentimental pieces such as *The Village Blacksmith* to his epic, and probably most recognisable work, *The Song of Hiawatha*. Longfellow was an historian, explorer and geologist who had the astounding ability of being able to express emotions in verse with seemingly little effort. It took him a year and a half to complete Hiawatha, completing it in November 1855. He was the son of Stephen Longfellow and Zilpah Wadsworth Longfellow and was raised in Portland, Maine in the United States. He was a bright student and went on to study languages, despite being pushed towards law by his father. He went on to become a teacher and opened the world of European literature to his students. He married Mary Storer Porter in 1831 and was appointed a professorship at Harvard in 1834. Unfortunately Mary died prematurely and the lonely Longfellow moved to Cambridge, where he spent the remainder of his life. He took a room at Craigie House overlooking the river, which was later given to him as a wedding present on his marriage to Frances Appleton. As time went buy Longfellow felt his teaching career was encroaching on his writing, and he devoted the rest of his life doing what he loved best – writing poetry. Longfellow died on 24 March 1882.

❧❦❧

RICHARD LOVELACE (1618–1657)

Richard Lovelace was the eldest son of Sir William Lovelace, who was killed in action in 1627. Richard was educated at Oxford and became a popular figure with King Charles I and Queen Henrietta Maria. In April 1642, Lovelace presented a Royalist petition to parliament in favour of restoring the Anglican bishops, but this petition landed him in prison. While there he wrote 'To Althea. From Prison'. Having lost his sweetheart, Lucy Sacherevell, to another man and ruined by his support of the royalists, Lovelace lived on charity and died in poverty in 1658. Sacherevell, whom Lovelace affectionately called *Lux casta*, was probably the main influence behind his poetry. He received a posthumous award for his poems entitled *Lucasta: Postume Poems* which were published the year after his death.

JOHN McRAE (1872–1918)

John McRae was born in Canada and educated at the McGill University. He became a doctor and when war broke out he was appointed as medical consultant to all the British armies in France, although he died before he was able to take up the position. McCrae served in the artillery during the Second Boer War, and upon his return was appointed professor of pathology at the University of Vermont, where he taught until 1911. His experiences as a surgeon in World War I, during the Battle of Ypres in particular, led him to write one of his most famous poems 'In Flanders Fields'. Many believed it was a memorium to his close friend Lieutenant Alexis Helmer who was killed by a German artillery shell. McRae died of pneumonia in January 1918.

WILFRED OWEN (1893–1918)

Wilfred Owen was born in Oswestry, Shropshire, the eldest of four children. The influence of his evangelical upbringing was clearly visible in his poems and their themes. In 1913, Owen moved to France and taught English in the Berlitz School of languages. He was enlisted into the Artists' Rifles in 1915, but the horrors of war left him shellshocked and he was sent to a war hospital near Edinburgh to convalesce. Owen returned to fight and was awarded the Military Cross for bravery at Amiens. Owen was killed on the 4 November 1918 whilst attempting to lead his men across the Sambre canal at Ors. His parents learned of his death on 11 November, armistice day.

MARGARET JUNKIN PRESTON (1820-1897)

Margaret Junkin Preston was the sister of Elinore Junkin Jackson, who was the first wife of Thomas Jonathan 'Stonewall' Jackson. Margaret formed a close bond with Jackson and remained close to him even after Elinore's death just 14 months after the wedding. Victorian principles stopped them from getting married, and Margaret eventually married Major John T. L. Preston. The Preston family, like many others, was divided by the American Civil War, and she wrote espousing the southern cause, writing some of the most popular verse in the Confederacy. After her children were grown up, Preston was able to devote more time to her writing before losing her eyesight in the late 1880s. After her husband's death in 1890, she moved to Baltimore to live with her son. She died peacefully in her sleep, fulfilling a wish to do so as expressed in her poem *Euthanasia*.

JOHN PUDNEY (1909–1977)

John Sleigh Pudney was born in Buckinghamshire. He worked as a radio producer and scriptwriter for the BBC and then as a war correspondent at the onset of World War II. He joined the RAF in 1940, but was also recruited by the British Government to write about the work of air crews so that the general public could appreciate the value of their services. After the war he became literary editor of *News Review* and then joined the publishers Putnam as a director in 1950. He had two books of verse published before the war, and his most famous poem 'For Johnny' was written on the back of an envelope during an air raid on London in 1941.

ISAAC ROSENBERG (1890–1918)

Isaac Rosenberg was born in Bristol, the son of Jewish immigrants. When he was seven, the family moved to London where Rosenberg was educated in the schools of the East End. He left school at the age of fourteen and became an apprentice engraver — a job that he never took to. Rosenberg had a passion for art and became an accomplished watercolourist. He also loved to write poetry, but ill health forced him to move to a warmer climate and he left for South Africa. There he lectured on art and managed to get some of his poems published in magazines. Rosenberg never settled away from London and he returned in 1915. The same year, keen to play his part in the war, Rosenberg joined the Bantams — a special battalion designed for men who were too short to be accepted by the other regiments. He spent two years fighting on the Western front and utilised his spare time in the trenches by writing poetry, including *Break of Day in the Trenches*. Rosenberg was killed on 1 April 1918 by a German raiding party, but his body was never recovered and his headstone still stands over an empty grave.

***

SIEGFRIED SASSOON (1886–1967)

Siegfried Sassoon loved books and literature from an early age and his talent for poetry was obvious in his early life. Before the outbreak of war, Sassoon published several small collections of poems, the most accomplished of which was a parody of Masefield called 'The Daffodil Murderer'. His patriotism prompted Sassoon to enlist in the army on the first day of the Great War. He was awarded the Military Cross — an honour he renounced. His experiences in the trenches and the misery of war completely transformed his writing. His polemic *A Soldier's Declaration*, told of the futility of war. He met fellow war poet, Wilfred Owen, when the two men had a brief spell in Craiglockhart Hospital suffering from the horrors of war. He continued to write in his later life and it was still apparent that this man was haunted by his time on the Western Front.

***

ALAN SEEGER (1888–1916)

Alan Seeger was born in New York and educated at Harvard. Despite being a bright student, after graduating he became what his parents described as 'a slob'. He sponged off his friends, became anti-social and took no pride in his appearance. To try and improve their son, the Seeger's sent Alan to Paris to continue his studies. When the war broke out,

Seeger saw it as a release from the drudgery of everyday life and rushed to join the French Foreign Legion. He dreamt of leading heroic charges in the thick of battle, but his escapades were cut short when he was killed on the fourth day of the Battle of the Somme on 4 July 1916. Seeger's poetry was not published until 1917, a year after his death and much reflected the young man's desire to die a glorious death in the throes of battle.

❧❧❧

WILLIAM SHAKESPEARE (1564–1616)

William Shakespeare is reknown for his dramas and poetic acting and is considered to be the greatest playwright of all time. He was born in England in Stratford-upon-Avon and married Anne Hathaway, the daughter of a farmer, in 1582. His poetry was published before his plays with two poems in 1593 and 1594, both dedicated to his patron Henry Wriothesley, the Earl of Southampton. At his height of writing, Shakespeare produced roughly two dramas a year, and his earliest plays include *Henry VI* and *A Midsummer Night's Dream*. For all his fame, William Shakespeare remains a man of mystery. There are so many gaps in his life that we still know very little about the great bard. The most famous of his war poems begins:

'Once more unto the breach, dear friends, once more,
Or close the wallup with our English dead!'

❧❧❧

KENNETH SLESSOR (1901–1971)

Kenneth Slessor was born in Orange, New South Wales. His first attempts at poetry were published in the *Bulletin* magazine while he was still at school. He made his career as a journalist writing for the *Sydney Sun, Melbourne Punch* and the *Melbourne Herald*. At the outbreak of World War II, Slessor was appointed an official war correspondent and spent his time with the Australian roops in England, Greece, the Middle East and New Guinea. When the war was over he returned to work for the *Sydney Sun* as literary editor, where he stayed until 1957. After this he worked for the *Daily Telegraph* and *Sunday Telegraph*. Slessor wrote most of his poems after World War II and his poem *Beach Burial* was a tribute to the Australian troops with whom he spent a lot of his war years. There is a poetry award called the Kenneth Slessor Prize for Poetry which is awarded annually for outstanding works.

CHARLES HAMILTON SORLEY (1895–1915)

Charles Hamilton Sorley was born in Aberdeen, the son of a professor of moral philosophy at Aberdeen University. An extremely bright student, Sorley won a scholarship to Marlborough College where he excelled at debating. After taking a year out in Germany, Sorley accepted an offer of a place at University College, Cambridge. When World War I broke out, Sorley immediately enlisted and joined the Suffolk Regiment as a 2nd Lieutenant. His unit was sent to the Western Front, and after just three months, Sorley was promoted to captain, but his career ended when he was shot down by a sniper at the Battle of Loos. As a legacy, Sorley left only 37 completed poems which were found in his kit bag after his death. A book of his poems entitled *Marlborough and Other Poems*, published posthumously, became a popular and critical success in 1916.

⁂

ALFRED, LORD TENNYSON (1809–1892)

Alfred Tennyson was a very influential poet in the Victorian era. He succeeded as Poet Laureate in 1850, taking over from William Wordsworth. Tennyson's childhood was unhappy, and lived with a morbid fear of mental illness. His family were afflicted with mental problems, and his brother had to be confined to an institution in 1843. In his late twenties, Tennyson himself became even more paranoid and his behaviour became abusive and violent. Tennyson went on to study at Trinity College, Cambridge, where he joined the literary club and made close friends with Arthur Hallam. This is where his love of poetry began and in 1830 he published *Chiefly Lyrical*. His major poetic achievements were after the death of Hallam and his most famous war poem is undoubtedly *The Charge of the Light Brigade*, published in *Maud* in 1855.

⁂

DYLAN THOMAS (1914–1954)

Dylan Thomas was born in Wales, the son of an English teacher at Swansea Grammar School. He started writing poetry as a schoolboy and his first job on leaving school was a reporter for the *South Wales Evening Post*. His first book of poetry entitled *Eighteen Poems* was published in 1934. After this Thomas moved to London where he worked in journalism, broadcasting and script writing. During World War II, Thomas lived in London, spending most of his time writing and broadcasting for the BBC. He was a conscientious objector who was totally opposed to killing in any shape or form. During this time he wrote some of his finest poems, and was invited to lecture in the United States. Prone to bouts of heavy drinking, Thomas's health started to decline and he died at the age of 39 – ostensibly of alcoholic poisoning – on 9 November 1953.

❧❧❧❀❧❧❧

EDWARD THOMAS (1878–1917)
Edward Thomas was born and Educated in Oxford and his first book was published when he was just 18 years old. He wrote over 30 books and many more articles and reviews. It was the American poet Robert Frost who first encouraged Thomas to write poetry and at the end of his career he had written as many as 144 poems. Many of his verses were darkly influenced by World War I, and most were sadly rejected which only added to his melancholy and severe depression. He volunteered for the front and went to France with the Royal Garrison Artillery at the end of January 1917. Sadly he was killed ten weeks later, leaving a wife and three children.

❧❧❧❀❧❧❧

KATHARINE TYNAN (1861–1931)
Katharine Tynan was born in Clondalkin, County Dublin and educated at Siena Convent, Drogheda. Her poems were first published in 1878 and Tynan went on to play an important

part in the literary circles of Dublin. After her marriage in 1898 to the writer and barrister Henry Albert Hinkson, Tynan usually wrote under the name Katharine Tynan Hinkson. During the war she had a son serving in Palestine and another in France. She became a close friend of W B Yeats. Besides her poetry, Tynan also wrote over 100 novels, five being autobiographical volumes. She died at the age of 70 while living in London.

WALT WHITMAN (1819–1892)

Walt or Walter Whitman was an American poet, journalist and essayist, who is best known for his *Leaves of Grass* in 1855. Born in Long Island, New York, Whitman went on to read classics and was inspired by writers such as Goethe, Hegel and Emerson. He wrote for and edited several periodicals in the mid-1800s but his dream was to write a new kind of poetry. Whitman struggled to support himself through most of his life and the first edition of *Leaves of Grass* appeared in July 1855 at Whitman's own expense. The book was about the poet's own experiences, including his homosexuality. During the American Civil War, Whitman worked as a clerk in Washington, surviving on a meagre salary and modest royalties. Much of his earnings went towards looking after his widowed mother and an invalid brother. His experiences certainly had a major effect on his writing. His most famous poem of this period was *O Captain! My Captain!* which was about the death of Lincoln. Whitman's final volume was the 'deathbed' edition of *Leaves of Grass,* which he prepared in 1891-92. Whitman died on 26 March 1892 in Camden, New Jersey.

WILLIAM WORDSWORTH (1770–1850)

William Wordsworth was born in Cumberland in the beautiful lake district, and the magnificent scenery of his birthplace had a great influence on his poetry. He studied at Cambridge and made his debut as a writer in 1787, when he published his first sonnet. Coleridge was also a major influence on his life and works, and stimulated by his love of nature Wordsworth published his first major work, *Lyrical Ballads* in 1798. In 1802, Wordsworth married his childhood sweetheart Mary Hutchinson, and together they had five children. He succeeded Robert Southey as England's Poet Laureate in 1842 and during his lifetime wrote over 70,0000 lines of verse. In 1823 he wrote a war poem entitled *Not love, not war, nor the tumultuous swell.*

WILLIAM BUTLER YEATS (1865–1939)

W. B. Yeats was born in Dublin and educated in both London and Dublin. During his early years of writing, his dramatic works were more prominent than his poetry. Together with Lady Gregory he founded the Irish Theatre and served as its chief playwright. Yeat's style changed dramatically after 1910, taking on a more poetical and abstract form. Yeats received an honorary degree from Trinity College, Dublin in 1922, the same year that the American Civil War broke out. He was elected to the Irish senate, but only served six years due to failing health. He is one of the few poets whose best works were written after the award of the Nobel Prize. Although he received the prize for his dramatic works, he is probably best remembered today for his poems, especially *The Tower* (1928) and *The Winding Stair* (1933). Yeats was often homesick for Ireland, and his poem *The Lake Isle of Innisfree* was written during one of these periods.

THE
AMERICAN
CIVIL WAR

Origins of the American Civil War

The American Civil War was one of the bloodiest hostilities ever fought in North America. Over 600,000 people died – not just on the battlefield, but from disease and exposure to the elements as well. In just two days more men fell on the fields of Shiloh in April 1862, than any other previous conflict in America.

The causes behind the American Civil War can be traced back to the early years of American colonisation. Prior to the Civil War, the roots of most of the conflicts in America revolved around the slave issue. The Civil War itself was no different, and came down to two issues – slavery and the preservation of the Union. The industrial North was starting to benefit from the boom, which was fuelled by cheap immigration labour. On the contrary, the sparsely-populated South had to rely on slaves. Northern politicians believed the use of slaves to be barbaric and wanted the practice stamped-out. The South clung to the belief that each individual state should be allowed to decide its own policies, and the difference of opinion between the two states led to a bitter conflict.

When it came to the actual reasons behind the fight, the majority of Confederates actually took up arms for the principle of their States' rights rather than their rights to keep slaves, and did everything to defend their territory from northern invasion. The North were primarily fighting to preserve the Union, but they also took the morality of slavery into the equation. The final straw that broke the camel's back, was the election of Abraham Lincoln as president in 1860. This was just too much for the southern states, who subsequently seceded from the Union to form the Confederate States of America. Soon the southerners were clamouring for war and the first guns were fired at 4.30 am on 12 April 1861. Confederate gunmen opened fire on Federal, managed to hold Fort Sumner, and the only fatal casualty of the day was one single horse. It is hard to believe that such a long and bloody war could begin with such a small and insignificant battle.

The Confederate States were sadly outnumbered by the strength of the industrial North. Although European troops did not get involved in the American Civil War, it is still estimated that as many as 50,000 Britons fought as volunteers on both sides. British companies also supplied arms to both sides, but primarily to the southern states. The North thought they had it in the bag, little did they know how hard they would have to fight to gain victory.

THE CONFLICT ITSELF

During the first year the battles were small. Ironically neither side could muster more than a small number of experienced troops who just managed to muddle their way through the fighting. However, those that survived the early battles went on to become some of the most experienced troops in the world. Needless to say huge numbers of less experienced soldiers lost their lives on the battlefields. Casualties were high due to the clash between modern and out-of-date weaponry, many being handled by novice volunteers. Most of the battles quickly degenerated into bloodbaths, each side firing randomly at the other until one or the other withdrew in defeat. It soon became an abominable war of attrition.

THE END OF THE CONFLICT

In 1864, the Union commander-in-chief Ulysses S. Grant, little by little squeezed the last bit of life out of the southerners, completely disregarding the number of casualties his forces suffered. The North had won and the Union was saved. Slavery would be abolished but at the cost of over half a million lives.

∞☙⚓☙∞

The poems in this section serve as reminders of the valiant souls who fought for their beliefs both from the North and the South and the brave volunteers who came to their aid. The words are both gripping and powerful from the opening battle at Fort Sumner to General Lee's surrender at Appomattox. No words can express the horror of a war that ripped a nation in half, but these poems tell tales of heroic deeds and hopefully bring solace in remembering those who lost their lives.

Bivouac On A Mountain Side

I see before me now a travelling army halting,
Below a fertile valley spread, with barns and the orchards of
    summer,
Behind, the terraced sides of a mountain, abrupt, in places
    rising high,
Broken, with rocks, with clinging cedars, with tall shapes
    dingily seen,
The numerous camp-fires scatter'd near and far, some away up
    on the mountain,
The shadowy forms of men and horses, looming, large-sized,
    flickering,
And all over the sky – the sky! far, far out of reach, studded,
    breaking out, the eternal stars.

Walt Whitman

The Bivouac In The Snow

Halt! – the march is over,
  Day is almost done;
Loose the cumbrous knapsack,
  Drop the heavy gun.
Chilled and wet and weary,
  Wander to and fro,
Seeking wood to kindle
  Fires amidst the snow.

Round the bright blaze gather,
  Heed not sleet or cold;
Ye are Spartan soldiers,
  Stout and brave and bold.
Never Xerxian army
  Yet subdued a foe
Who but asked a blanket
  On a bed of snow.

Shivering, 'midst the darkness,
  Christian men are found,
There devoutly kneeling
  On the frozen ground –
Pleading for their country,
  In its hour of woe –
For the soldiers marching
  Shoeless through the snow.

Lost in heavy slumbers,
  Free from toil and strife,
Dreaming of their dear ones –
  Home, and child, and wife –
Tentless they are lying,
  While the fires burn low –
Lying in their blankets
  'Midst December's snow.

Margaret Junkin Preston

O Captain! My Captain!

O Captain! my Captain! our fearful trip is done,
The ship has weathered every rack, the prize we sought is won,
The port is near, the bells I hear, the people all exulting,
While follow eyes the steady keel, the vessel grim and daring;
But O heart! heart! heart!
O the bleeding drops of red,
Where on the deck my Captain lies,
Fallen cold and dead.

O Captain! my Captain! rise up and hear the bells;
Rise up – for you the flag is flung – for you the bugle trills,
For you bouquets and ribboned wreaths – for you the shores
  a-crowding,
For you they call, the swaying mass, their eager faces turning;
Here Captain! dear father!
This arm beneath your head!
It is some dream that on the deck
You've fallen cold and dead.

My captain does not answer, his lips are pale and still,
My father does not feel my arm, he has no pulse nor will,
The ship is anchored safe and sound, its voyage closed and done,
From fearful trip the victor ship comes in with object won;
Exult, O shores, and ring O bells!
But I, with mournful tread,
Walk the deck my Captain lies,
Fallen cold and dead.

Walt Whitman

The Blue And The Gray

By the flow of the inland river,
  Whence the fleets of iron have fled,
Where the blades of the grave-grass quiver,
  Asleep are the ranks of the dead:
Under the sod and the dew,
  Waiting the judgment-day;
Under the one, the Blue,
  Under the other, the Gray

These in the robings of glory,
  Those in the gloom of defeat,
All with the battle-blood gory,
  In the dusk of eternity meet:
Under the sod and the dew,
  Waiting the judgement-day
Under the laurel, the Blue,
  Under the willow, the Gray.

From the silence of sorrowful hours
  The desolate mourners go,
Lovingly laden with flowers
  Alike for the friend and the foe;

Under the sod and the dew,
  Waiting the judgement-day;
Under the roses, the Blue,
  Under the lilies, the Gray.

So with an equal splendor,
  The morning sun-rays fall,
With a touch impartially tender,
  On the blossoms blooming for all:
Under the sod and the dew,
  Waiting the judgment-day;
Broidered with gold, the Blue,
  Mellowed with gold, the Gray.

So, when the summer calleth,
  On forest and field of grain,
With an equal murmur falleth
  The cooling drip of the rain:
Under the sod and the dew,
  Waiting the judgment -day,
Wet with the rain, the Blue
  Wet with the rain, the Gray.

Sadly, but not with upbraiding,
  The generous deed was done,
In the storm of the years that are
    fading
  No braver battle was won:
Under the sod and the dew,
  Waiting the judgment-day;
Under the blossoms, the Blue,
  Under the garlands, the Gray

No more shall the war cry sever,
  Or the winding rivers be red;
They banish our anger forever
  When they laurel the graves of our
    dead!
Under the sod and the dew,
  Waiting the judgment-day,
Love and tears for the Blue,
  Tears and love for the Gray.

Francis Miles Finch

An Army Corps on the March

With its cloud of skirmishers in advance,
With now the sound of a single shot snapping like a whip, and
    now an irregular volley,
The swarming ranks press on and on, the dense brigades press on,
Gliterring dimly, toiling under the sun – the dust-cover'd men,
In columns rise and fall to the undulations of the ground,
With artillery interspers'd – the wheels rumble, the horses sweat,
As the army corps advances.

Walt Whitman

Killed at the Ford

He is dead, the beautiful youth,
  The heart of honour, the tongue of truth,
He, the life and light of us all,
  Whose voice was blithe as a bugle-call,
Whom all eyes followed with one consent,
  The cheer of whose laugh, and whose pleasant word,
Hushed all murmurs of discontent.

Sudden and swift a whistling ball
  Came out of a wood, and the voice was still;
Something I heard in the darkness fall,
  And for a moment my blood grew chill;
I spake in a whisper, as he who speaks
  In a room where some one is lying dead;
But he made no answer to what I said.

We lifted him up to his saddle again,
  And through the mire and the mist and the rain
Carried him back to the silent camp,
  And laid him as if asleep on his bed;
And I saw by the light of the surgeon's lamp
  Two white roses upon his cheeks,
And one, just over his heart, blood-red!

Henry Wadsworth Longfellow

39

The
Boer War

Origins of the Boer War

The Boer War was the name given to the South African conflicts which took place between 1880–81 and again in 1899–1902. The war was fought between the British and the descendants of the Dutch settlers (or Boers). At the time there was a lot of political unrest between the two sides. The Boers treated the blacks abominably and ignored all basic human rights. They forced them to pay taxes, but were not prepared to give them the right to vote. This treatment infuriated the British, who had abolished slavery in all its colonies in 1834, while the Boers made it clear they wanted to keep their slaves.

Adding to the slave problem was the fact that the British had already seized Swaziland, Bechuanaland and Basutoland in Africa, which basically meant they had the Boers surrounded. They feared if the British claimed any more territory the Boers would have no way out, particularly as the British had made it clear that they wanted to take control of all of Southern Africa.

There were also economical reasons for the war. The Boers had taken control of the Transvaal and set up the Orange Free State. They had made the discovery of gold and diamonds in the Transvaal which made the area very economically viable and the British and the Boers started to argue about their boundaries.

One of the individuals who played a major role in provoking the war, was Cecil John Rhodes, an English-born businessman, mining magnate, and politician in South Africa. He was a staunch imperialist and strove to expand the British empire further. He was very anti-Boer and his opinions went a long way in influencing the powers back home. Sir

Alfred Milner, was the British High Commissioner for South Africa and Governor of the Cape Colony between 1897 and 1899, when the Boer War broke out. He was also strongly anti-Boer and, although he was supposed to be a peacemaker, the demands he put on the Boers actually helped to spark the war. The final character instrumental in aggravating the situation was the Colonial Secretary, Joseph Chamberlain. He was seen as the leader of the radicals with his calls for land reform and higher taxes on the rich, but he was also a supporter of Imperialism. At the time of the Boer War he was primarily responsible for British foreign policy.

The Boers, under the leadership of Paul Kruger – the President of the Transvaal – resented the colonial policy of both Chamberlain and Milner, fearing that the Transvaal would lose its independence. Kruger ordered the first attack against the British in 1881. The British were infuriated by the Boer's first assault, and the early defeat of the British led the arrogant Boers to believe that they could overcome their forces with ease.

The Boers managed a series of successes even though they only had 88,000 soldiers. They had received military equipment from Germany, added to this the Boers were led by some outstanding soldiers such as Louis Botha and Jan Smuts, and they successfully besieged the British garrisons at Ladysmith, Mafeking and Kimberley.

Aware that they needed some backup, the British sent for reinforcements in 1900. This gave them the power to take control of the Boer capital, Petroria on 5 June. For the next couple of years, the Boer soldiers raided isolated British units in South Africa and Lord Kitchener retaliated by destroying Boer farms and moving many of the civilians into concentration camps.

The British action in South Africa received strong opposition from many of the leading Liberal politicians and the majority of the Independent Labour Party, describing it as one of the worst examples of Imperialism they had witnessed. The Boer War came to its conclusion with the signing of the Treaty of Vereeniging in May 1902. This peace treaty brought to an end the Boer republics of Transvaal and the Orange Free State, but they did receive £3 million from the British to restock their farms and rebuild their damaged land. They were eventually granted self-government in 1907.

In South Africa, President Kruger received a lot of international sympathy which bolstered his political standing. Cecil Rhodes was forced to retire as prime minister of the Cape Colony and never regained his political prominence. The second part of the Boer War left lasting shadows of the history of South Africa. The devastation of both Boer and black African populations in the concentration camps had a lasting effect on the demography and the quality of life in the area. Many of the prisoners were unable to return to their farms because of the effect of the scorched earth policy of Roberts and Kitchener. This refers to the practice of burning crops to deny the enemy their food sources. This left many destitute Boers and black Africans competing with the Uitlanders (or foreign migrant workers) fighting for the precious jobs in the mines.

⸲⸱⸲

The poet most synonymous with the Boer War was Rudyard Kipling, who tried to apologise for the aggression of Imperialism. This made him a popular target for the pro-Boer press. Kipling's talent lay in his understanding of sentiments and being able to express them in verse.

Drummer Hodge

They throw in Drummer Hodge, to rest
  Uncoffined – just as found:
His landmark is a kopje-crest
  That breaks the veldt around;
And foreign constellations west
  Each night above his mound.

Young Hodge the Drummer never knew –
  Fresh from his Wessex home –
The meaning of the broad Karoo,
  The Bush, the dusty loam,
And why uprose to nightly view
  Strange stars amid the gloam.

Yet portion of that unknown plain
  Will Hodge forever be;
His homely Northern breast and brain
  Grow to some Southern tree,
And strange-eyed constellation reign
  His stars eternally.

Thomas Hardy

45

Ubique

There is a word you often see, pronounce it as you may -
  'You bike,' 'you bikwe,' 'ubbikwe' - alludin' to R.A.
It serves 'Orse, Field, an' Garrison as motto for a crest,
  An' when you've found out all it means I'll tell you 'alf the rest.

Ubique means the long-range Krupp be'ind the low-range 'ill -
  Ubique means you'll pick it up an', while you do stand, still.
Ubique means you've caught the flash an' timed it by the sound.
  Ubique means five gunners' 'ash before you've loosed a round.

Ubique means Blue Fuse, an' make the 'ole to sink the trail.
  Ubique means stand up an' take the Mauser's 'alf-mile 'ail.
Ubique means the crazy team not God nor man can 'old.
  Ubique means that 'orse's scream which turns your innards cold.

Ubique means 'Bank, 'Olborn, Bank - a penny all the way -
  The soothin' jingle-bump-an'-clank from day to peaceful day.
Ubique means 'They've caught De Wet, an' now we sha'n't be long.'
  Ubique means 'I much regret, the beggar's going strong!'

Ubique means the tearin' drift where, breech-blocks jammed with mud,
  The khaki muzzles duck an' lift across the khaki flood.
Ubique means the dancing plain that changes rocks to Boers.
  Ubique means the mirage again an' shellin' all outdoors.

Ubique means 'Entrain at once for Grootdefeatfontein'!
  Ubique means 'Off-load your guns' - at midnight in the rain!
Ubique means 'More mounted men. Return all guns to store.'
  Ubique means the R.A.M.R. Infantillery Corps!

Ubique means the warnin' grunt the perished linesman knows,
  When o'er 'is strung an' sufferin' front the shrapnel sprays 'is foes,
An' as their firin' dies away the 'usky whisper runs
  From lips that 'aven't drunk all day: 'The Guns! Thank Gawd, the Guns!'

Extreme, depressed, point-blank or short, end-first or any'ow,
  From Colesberg Kop to Quagga's Poort - from Ninety-Nine till now -

There's nothin' this side 'Eaven or 'Ell Ubique doesn't mean!

Rudyard Kipling

Tommy

I went into a public-'ouse to get a pint o' beer,
  The publican 'e up an' sez, "We serve no red-coats here."
The girls be'ind the bar they laughed an' giggled fit to die,
  I outs into the street again an' to myself sez I:
O it's Tommy this, an' Tommy that, an' "Tommy, go away";
  But it's "Thank you, Mister Atkins", when the band begins to play,
The band begins to play, my boys, the band begins to play,
  O it's "Thank you, Mister Atkins", when the band begins to play.

I went into a theatre as sober as could be,
  They gave a drunk civilian room, but 'adn't none for me;
They sent me to the gallery or round the music-'alls,
  But when it comes to fightin', Lord! they'll shove me in the stalls!
For it's Tommy this, an' Tommy that, an' "Tommy, wait outside";
  But it's "Special train for Atkins" when the trooper's on the tide,
The troopship's on the tide, my boys, the troopship's on the tide,
  O it's "Special train for Atkins" when the trooper's on the tide.

Yes, makin' mock o' uniforms that guard you while you sleep
  Is cheaper than them uniforms, an' they're starvation cheap;
An' hustlin' drunken soldiers when they're goin' large a bit
  Is five times better business than paradin' in full kit.

Then it's Tommy this, an' Tommy that, an' "Tommy, 'ow's yer soul?"
  But it's "Thin red line of 'eroes" when the drums begin to roll,
The drums begin to roll, my boys, the drums begin to roll,
  O it's "Thin red line of 'eroes" when the drums begin to roll.

We aren't no thin red 'eroes, nor we aren't no blackguards too,
  But single men in barricks, most remarkable like you;
An' if sometimes our conduck isn't all your fancy paints,
  Why, single men in barricks don't grow into plaster saints;
While it's Tommy this, an' Tommy that, an' "Tommy, fall be'ind",
  But it's "Please to walk in front, sir", when there's trouble in the wind,
There's trouble in the wind, my boys, there's trouble in the wind,
  O it's "Please to walk in front, sir", when there's trouble in the wind.

You talk o' better food for us, an' schools, an' fires, an' all:
  We'll wait for extra rations if you treat us rational.
Don't mess about the cook-room slops, but prove it to our face
  The Widow's Uniform is not the soldier-man's disgrace.
For it's Tommy this, an' Tommy that, an' "Chuck him out, the brute!"
  But it's "Saviour of 'is country" when the guns begin to shoot;
An' it's Tommy this, an' Tommy that, an' anything you please;
  An' Tommy ain't a bloomin' fool – you bet that Tommy sees!

Rudyard Kipling

A Wife in London

I The Tragedy

She sits in the tawny vapour
  That the City lanes have uprolled,
Behind whose webby fold on fold
  Like a waning taper
The street-lamp glimmers cold.

A messenger's knock cracks smartly,
  Flashed news is in her hand
Of meaning it dazes to understand
  Though shaped so shortly:
He – has fallen – in the far South Land . . .

II The Irony

'Tis the morrow; the fog hangs thicker,
  The postman nears and goes:
A letter is brought whose lines disclose
  By the firelight flicker
His hand, whom the worm now knows:

Fresh – firm – penned in highest feather –
  Page-full of his hoped return,
And of home-planned jaunts by brake and burn
  In the summer weather,
And of new love that they would learn.

Thomas Hardy

Untitled

The glamour gone, some scattered graves and memories dim remain:
With his old pals across the field, he'll never trek again;
But yet there's nothing he regrets as he awaits his Call,
For what was done or lost or won, he did his bit – that's all.

Sergeant 4486

WORLD WAR I

Origins of World War I

The reasons behind the onset of the Great War as it has become known, are complicated. Frustrations and animosity had been building up for many years, but the spark which kindled the fire was the assassination of Archduke Franz Ferdinand on 28 June 1914. He was the heir to the Austro-Hungarian throne, and his death at the hands of the Black Hand (a Serbian nationalist secret society) outside Sarajevo's Town Hall, set in motion a series of events that culminated in the world's first global war.

Following the assassination the Serbs started to make demands to have their people freed and that Bosnia was handed back. Austria–Hungary's first reaction was to fight back, but they were cautious because they knew that Russia would probably get embroiled in the conflict due to the number of Slavs living in Russia. They decided to go to Germany and ask for their backing.

Germany agreed to support Austria–Hungary, so they went to Serbia with a list of demands, knowing full well that they would be rejected. By 28 July the Keizer had given his full backing for the war and gave orders to attack immediately. From here the conflict spiralled out of control, as Germany decided to go to war with Russia in accordance with the Triple Alliance. The Triple Alliance was a military alliance between Germany, Austria-Hungary and Italy, in which each member promised mutual support in the event of an attack by any two other great powers. By the 3 August, the situation was getting really serious and Germany declared war on France.

Britain became involved on the 5 August, and the First World War had begun.

Of course, the assassination of Franz Ferdinand was not the only cause of the war, just a small part – colonial rivalry was also a contributary factor. Most of the European powers, with the exception of Austria and Russia, had colonies in Africa, which caused much rivalry over the territories. For example, Italy turned to Germany and Austria when she lost Tunis to France in 1881. Germany, aware that they didn't have a strong naval position, set to building more battleships which caused more rivalry with Britain. Eventually the frustration overflowed and the world was at war.

As the war progressed the Germans starting to lose power and their armies were unable to sustain any more damage as they started to run out of supplies. In August 1918, the Allied forces broke through Germany's defences and managed to turn the odds in their favour.

World War I was a long and bitter conflict which caused a lot of suffering. Not only were loved ones killed, but many people lost their homes or were left permanently disabled. It was not a fight using just sticks and spears, but a far more advanced type of warfare with automatic machine guns, submarines, tanks and poisonous gas, all of which left devastation in their wake, causing the deaths of millions of people. The political order of Europe was destroyed and the German, Austro–Hungarian and Russian empires ceased to exist. It wasn't long before the Ottoman Empire crumbled as well. New nations started to emerge, borders were radically shifted and other minor conflicts between the races started to erupt. Having faced four years of economic ruin and material devastation, the world had to work out how to make a recovery. Somewhere in the midst of this chaos, the leaders of the victorious coalition assembled in Paris in January 1919 and set about forging a new international system. They knew that the decisions they made would determine the future of Europe and much of the rest of the world as well. The result was the Treaty of Versailles headed by the powerful leaders — Prime Minister David Lloyd George of Britain, Prime Minister Vittorio Orlando of Italy, Premier Georges Clemenceau of France and President Woodrow Wilson of the United States. Germany was compelled to sign the treaty on 28 June 1919, unilaterally disarmed and forced to give up its colonial empire. They also had to accept responsibility for the outbreak of World War I and pay the cost of the reparations.

⤜⟊⤛

More than any other war, World War I inspired writers and poets of all generations and classes, most notably among those that were directly involved in the fighting. Many outstanding poems were produced, chiefly in the form of personal memoir. For many of us it is hard to imagine that something truly poetic can come out of something so abominable as war. For those people who have been affected by its destructive force, these poems will have extra meaning. The poetry of Wilfred Owen, Siefried Sassoon and Charlotte Mew, to name just a few, capture the truth of the bitter conflict and engage the reader in an absorbing and compelling way.

No One Cares Less Than I

'No one cares less than I,
   Nobody knows but God,
Whether I am destined to lie
   Under a foreign clod,'
Were the words I made to the bugle call in the morning.

But laughing, storming, scorning,
   Only the bugles know
What the bugles say in the morning,
   And they do not care, when they blow
The call that I heard and made words to early this morning.

Edward Thomas

To His Love

He's gone, and all our plans
   Are useless indeed.
We'll walk no more on Cotswold
   Where the sheep feed
Quietly and take no heed.

His body that was so quick
   Is not as you
Knew it, on Severn river
   Under the blue
Driving our small boat through.

You would not know him now . . .
   But still he died
Nobly, so cover him over
   With violets of pride
Purple from Severn side.

Cover him, cover him soon!
   And with thick-set
Masses of memoried flowers –
   Hide that red wet
Thing I must somehow forget.

Ivor Gurney

Trenches: St Eloi

Over the flat slope of St Eloi
   A wide wall of sand bags.
Night.
   In the silence desultory men
Pottering over small fires, cleaning their mess-tins:
   To and fro, from the lines,
Men walk as on Piccadill,
   Making paths in the dark,
Through scattered dead horses,
   Over a dead Belgian's belly.

The Germans have rockets. The English have no rockets.
Behind the line, cannon, hidden, lying back miles.
Before the lines, chaos:

My mind is a corridor. The minds about me are corridors.
Nothing suggests itself. There is nothing to do but keep on.

T. E. Hulme

A Girl's Song

The Meuse and Marne have little waves;
    The slender poplars o'er them lean.
One day they will forget the graves
    That give the grass its living green.

Some brown French girl the rose will wear
    That springs above his comely head;
Will twine it in her russet hair,
    Nor wonder why it is so red.

His blood is in the rose's veins,
    His hair is in the yellow corn.
My grief is in the weeping rains
    And in the keening wind forlorn.

Flow softly, softly, Marne and Meuse;
    Tread lightly all ye browsing sheep;
Fall tenderly, O silver dews,
    For here my dear Love lies asleep.

The earth is on his sealèd eyes,
    The beauty marred that was my pride;
Would I were lying where he lies,
    And sleeping sweetly by his side!

The Spring will come by Meuse and Marne,
    The birds be blithesome in the tree.
I heap the stones to make his cairn
    Where many sleep as sound as he.

Katharine Tynan

First Time In

After the dread tales and red yarns of the Line
    Anything might have come to us; but the divine
Afterglow brought us up to a Welsh colony
    Hiding in sandbag ditches, whispering consolatory
Soft foreign things. Then we were taken in
    To low cuts candle-lit, shaded close by slitten
Oilsheets, and there the boys gave us kind welcome,
    So that we looked out as from the edge of home.
Sang us Welsh things, and changed all former notions
    To human hopeful things. And the next day's guns
Nor any line-pangs ever quite could blot out
    That strangely beautiful entry to war's rout;
Candles they gave us, precious and shared over-rations –
    Ulysses found little more in his wanderings without doubt.
'David of the White Rock', the 'Slumber Song' so soft, and that
    Beautiful tune to which roguish words by Welsh pit boys
Are sung – but never more beautiful than there
    under the gun's noise.

Ivor Gurney

A Private

This ploughman dead in battle slept out of doors
    Many a frozen night, and merrily
Answered staid drinkers, good bedmen, and all bores"
    'At Mrs Greenland's Hawthurn Bush,' said he,
'I slept.' None knew which bush. Above the town,
    Beyond 'The Drover,' a hundred spot the down
In Wiltshire. And where now at last he sleeps
    More sound in France – that, too, he secret keeps.

Edward Thomas

The Soldier

If I should die, think only this of me:
    That there's some corner of a foreign field
That is for ever England. There shall be
    In that rich earth a richer dust concealed;
A dust whom England bore, shaped, made aware,
    Gave, once, her flowers to love, her ways to roam,
A body of England's, breathing English air,
    Washed by the rivers, blest by suns of home.

And think, this heart, all evil shed away,
    A pulse in the eternal mind, no less
Gives somewhere back the thoughts by England given;
    Her sights and sounds; dreams happy as her day;
And laughter, learnt of friends; and gentleness,
    In hearts at peace, under an English heaven.

Rupert Brooke

An Irish Airman Foresees His Death

I know that I shall meet my fate
  Somewhere among the clouds above;
Those that I fight I do not hate,
  Those that I guard I do not love;
My country is Kiltartan Cross,
  My countrymen Kiltartan's poor,
No likely end could bring them loss
  Or leave them happier than before.
Nor law, nor duty bade me fight,
  Nor public men, nor cheering crowds,
A lonely impulse of delight
  Drove to this tumult in the clouds;
I balanced all, brought all to mind,
  The years to come seemed waste of breath,
A waste of breath the years behind
  In balance with this life, this death.

W. B. Yeats

Long Ages Past

Long ages past in Egypt thou wert worshipped
    And thou wert wrought from ivory and beryl.
They brought thee jewels and they brought their slain,
    Thy feet were dark with blood of sacrifice.
From dawn to midnight, O my painted idol,
    Thou satest smiling, and the noise of killing
Was harp and timbrel in thy pale jade ears;
    The livid dead were given thee for toys.

Thou wert a mad slave in a Persian palace,
    And the King loved thee for thy furious beauty,
And all men heard thy ravings with a smile
    Because thy face was fairer than a flower.
But with a little knife so wantonly
    Thou slewest women and thy pining lovers,
And on thy lips the stain of crimson blood,
    And on thy brow the pallor of their death.

Thou art the dream beheld by frenzied princes
     In smoke of opium. Thou art the last fulfilment
Of all the wicked, and of all the beautiful.
     We hold thee as a poppy to our mouths,
Finding with thee forgetfulness of God.
     Thou art the face reflected in a mirror
Of wild desire, of pain, of bitter pleasure.
     The witches shout thy name beneath the moon.
The fires of Hell have held thee in their fangs.

Wilfred Owen

Men Who March Away

What of the faith and fire within us
  Men who march away
Ere the barn-cocks say
  Night is growing gray,
To hazards whence no tears can win us;
  What of the faith and fire within us
Men who march away!

Is it a purblind prank, O think you,
  Friend with the musing eye
Who watch us stepping by,
  With doubt and dolorous sigh?
Can much pondering so hoodwink you?
  Is it a purblind prank, O think you,
Friend with the musing eye?

Nay. We see well what we are doing,
  Though some may not see –
Dalliers as they be –

England's need are we;
Her distress would leave us rueing:
  Nay. We well see what we are doing,
Though some may not see!

In our heart of hearts believing
  Victory crowns the just,
And that braggarts must
  Surely bite the dust,
Press we to the field ungrieving,
  In our heart of hearts believing
Victory crowns the just.

Hence the faith and fire within us
  Men who march away
Ere the barn-cocks say
  Night is growing gray,
To hazards whence no tears can win us;
  Hence the faith and fire within us
Men who march away.

Thomas Hardy

In Flanders Fields

In Flanders fields the poppies blow
  Between the crosses, row on row,
That mark our place; and in the sky
  The larks, still bravely singing, fly
Scarce heard amid the guns below.

We are the Dead. Short days ago
  We lived, felt dawn, saw sunset glow,
Loved and were loved, and now we lie
  In Flanders fields.

Take up our quarrel with the foe:
  To you from failing hands we throw
The torch; be yours to hold it high.
  If ye break faith with us who die
We shall not sleep, though poppies grow
  In Flanders fields.

John McCrae

Elegy in a Country Churchyard

The men that worked for England
   They have their graves at home:
And bees and birds of England
   About the cross can roam.

But they that fought for England,
   Following a falling star,
Alas, alas for England
   They have their graves afar.

And they that rule in England,
   In stately conclave met,
Alas, alas for England
   They have no graves as yet.

G. K. Chesterton

I Have a Rendezvous with Death

I have a rendezvous with Death
  At some disputed barricade,
When Spring comes back with rustling shade
  And apple-blossoms fill the air
I have a rendezvous with Death
  When Spring brings back blue days and fair.

It may be he shall take my hand
  And lead me into his dark land
And close my eyes and quench my breath
  It may be I shall pass him still.
I have a rendezvous with Death
  On some scarred slope of battered hill,
When Spring comes round again this year
  And the first meadow-flowers appear.

God knows 'twere better to be deep
  Pillowed in silk and scented down,
Where Love throbs out in blissful sleep,
  Pulse nigh to pulse, and breath to breath,
Where hushed awakenings are dear...
  But I've a rendezvous with Death
At midnight in some flaming town,
  When Spring trips north again this year,
And I to my pledged word am true,
  I shall not fail that rendezvous.

Alan Seeger

Bombardment

The Town has opened to the sun,
 Like a flat red lily with a million petals
She unfolds, she comes undone.

A sharp sky brushes upon
 The myriad glittering chimney-tips
As she gently exhales to the sun.

Hurrying creatures run
 Down the labyrinth of the sinister flower.
What is it they shun?

A dark bird falls from the sun,
 It curves in a rush to the heart of the vast
Flower: the day has begun.

D. H. Lawrence

The Silent One

Who died on the wires, and hung there, one of two –
Who for his hours of life had chattered through
Infinite lovely chatter of Bucks accent:
Yet faced unbroken wires; stepped over, and went
A noble fool, faithful to his stripes – and ended.
But I weak, hungry, and willing only for the chance
Of line – to fight in the line, lay down under unbroken
Wires, and saw the flashes and kept unshaken,
Till the politest voice – a finicking accent, said:
'Do you think you might crawl through there: there's a hole.'
Darkness, shot at: I smiled, as politely replied –
'I'm afraid not, Sir.' There was no hole no way to be seen
Nothing but chance of death, after tearing of clothes.
Kept flat, and watched the darkness, hearing bullets whizzing –
And thought of music – and swore deep heart's oaths
(Polite to God) and retreated and came on again,
Again retreated – a second time faced the screen.

Ivor Gurney

Rondeau of the Conscientious Objector

The hours have tumbled their leaden, monotonous sands
　And piled them up in a dull grey heap in the West.
I carry my patience sullenly through the waste lands;
　To-morrow will pour them all back, the dull hours I detest.

I force my cart through the sodden filth that is pressed
　Into ooze, and the sombre dirt spouts up at my hands
As I make my way in twilight now to rest.
　The hours have tumbled their leaden, monotonous sands.

A twisted thorn-tree still in the evening stands
　Defending the memory of leaves and the happy round nest.
But mud has flooded the homes of these weary lands
　And piled them up in a dull grey heap in the West.

All day has the clank of iron on iron distressed
  The nerve-bare place. Now a little silence expands
And a gasp of relief. But the soul is still compressed:
  I carry my patience sullenly through the waste lands.

The hours have ceased to fall, and a star commands
  Shadows to cover our stricken manhood, and blest
Sleep to make us forget: but he understands:
  To-morrow will pour them all back, the dull hours I detest.

D. H. Lawrence

Joining the Colours

There they go marching all in step so gay!
Smooth-cheeked and golden, food for shells and guns.
Blithely they go as to a wedding day,
    The mothers' sons.

The drab street stares to see them row on row
On the high tram-tops, singing like the lark.
Too careless-gay for courage, singing they go
    Into the dark.

With tin whistles, mouth-organs, any noise,
They pipe the way to glory and the grave;
Foolish and young, the gay and golden boys
    Love cannot save.

High heart! High courage! The poor girls they kissed
Run with them : they shall kiss no more, alas!
Out of the mist they stepped-into the mist
    Singing they pass.

Katharine Tynan

Last Words

'O Jesus Christ!' one fellow sighed.
And kneeled, and bowed, tho' not in prayer, and died.
    And the Bullets sang 'In Vain',
    Machine Guns chuckled 'Vain',
    Big Guns guffawed 'In Vain'.

'Father and mother!' one boy said.
Then smiled – at nothing, like a small child; being dead.
    And the Shrapnel Cloud
    Slowly gestured 'Vain',
    The falling splinters muttered 'Vain'.

'My love!' another cried, 'My love, my bud!'
Then, gently lowered, his whole face kissed the mud.
    And the flares gesticulated, 'Vain'.
    The Shells hooted, 'In Vain',
    And the Gas hissed, 'In Vain'.

Wilfred Owen

The General

'Good-morning; good-morning!' the General said
   When we met him last week on our way to the line.
Now the soldiers he smiled at are most of 'em dead,
   And we're cursing his staff for incompetent swine.
He's a cheery old card,' grunted Harry to Jack
   As they slogged up to Arras with rifle and pack.

But he did for them both by his plan of attack.

Siegfried Sassoon

Gethsemane 1914–1918

The Garden called Gethsemane
  In Picardy it was,
And there the people came to see
  The English soldiers pass.
We used to pass – we used to pass
  Or halt, as it might be,

And ship our masks in case of gas
  Beyond Gethsemane.

The Garden called Gethsemane,
  It held a pretty lass,
But all the time she talked to me
  I prayed my cup might pass.
The officer sat on the chair,
  The men lay on the grass,
And all the time we halted there

I prayed my cup might pass.
It didn't pass – it didn't pass –
  It didn't pass from me.
I drank it when we met the gas
  Beyond Gethsemane.

Rudyard Kipling

Greater Love

Red lips are not so red
   As the stained stones kissed by the English dead.
Kindness of wooed and wooer
Seems shame to their love pure.
O Love, your eyes lose lure
   When I behold eyes blinded in my stead!

Your slender attitude
   Trembles not exquisite like limbs knife-skewed,
Rolling and rolling there
Where God seems not to care;
Till the fierce Love they bear
   Cramps them in death's extreme decrepitude.

Your voice sings not so soft, –
  Though even as wind murmuring through raftered loft, –
Your dear voice is not dear,
Gentle, and evening clear,
As theirs whom none now hear
  Now earth has stopped their piteous mouths that coughed.

Heart, you were never hot,
  Nor large, nor full like hearts made great with shot;
And though your hand be pale,
Paler are all which trail
Your cross through flame and hail:
  Weep, you may weep, for you may touch them not.

Wilfred Owen

'Blighters'

The House is crammed: tier beyond tier they grin
    And cackle at the Show, while prancing ranks
Of harlots shrill the chorus, drink with din;
    'We're sure the Kaiser loves our dear old Tanks!'

I'd like to see a Tank come down the stalls,
    Lurching to rag-time tunes, or 'Home, sweet Home',
And there'd be no more jokes in Music-halls
    To mock the riddled corpses round Bapaume.

Siegfried Sassoon

Inspection

'You! What d'you mean by this?' I rapped.
   'You dare come on parade like this?'
'Please, sir, it's -' ' 'Old yer mouth,' the sergeant snapped.
 'I takes 'is name, sir?' - 'Please, and then dismiss.'

Some days 'confined to camp' he got,
  For being 'dirty on parade'.
He told me, afterwards, the damned spot
  Was blood, his own. 'Well, blood is dirt,' I said.

'Blood's dirt,' he laughed, looking away
  Far off to where his wound had bled
And almost merged for ever into clay.
  'The world is washing out its stains,' he said.
'It doesn't like our cheeks so red:
  Young blood's its great objection.
But when we're duly white-washed, being dead,
  The race will bear Field-Marshal God's inspection.'

Wilfred Owen

Reconciliation

When you are standing at your hero's grave,
 or near some homeless village where he died,
Remember, through your heart's rekindling pride,
 The German soldiers who were loyal and brave.

Men fought like brutes; and hideous things were done;
 And you have nourished hatred, harsh and blind.
But in that Golgotha perhaps you'll find
 The mothers of the men who killed your son.

Siegfried Sassoon

Often When Warring

Often when warring for he wist not what,
    An enemy-soldier, passing by one weak,
Has tendered water, wiped the burning cheek,
    And cooled the lips so black and clammed and hot;

Then gone his way, and maybe quite forgot
    The deed of grace amid the roar and reek;
Yet larger vision than loud arms bespeak
    He there has reached, although he has known it not

For natural mindsight, triumphing in the act
    Over the throes of artificial rage,
Has thuswise muffled victory's peal of pride,
    Rended to ribands policy's specious page
That deals but with evasion, code, and pact,
    And war's apology wholly stultified.

Thomas Hardy

This is No Case of Petty Right or Wrong

This is no case of petty right or wrong
   That politicians or philosophers
Can judge. I hate not Germans, nor grow hot
   With love of Englishmen, to please newspapers.
Beside my hate for one fat patriot
   My hatred of the Kaiser is love true:–
A kind of god he is, banging a gong.
   But I have not to choose between the two,
Or between justice and injustice. Dinned
   With war and argument I read no more
Than in the storm smoking along the wind
   Athwart the wood. Two witches' cauldrons roar.
From one the weather shall rise clear and gay;
   Out of the other an England beautiful
And like her mother that died yesterday.

Little I know or care if, being dull,
   I shall miss something that historians
Can rake out of the ashes when perchance
   The phoenix broods serene above their ken.
But with the best and meanest Englishmen
   I am one in crying, God save England, lest
We lose what never slaves and cattle blessed.
   The ages made her that made us from dust:
She is all we know and live by, and we trust
   She is good and must endure, loving her so:
And as we love ourselves we hate our foe.

Edward Thomas

For the Fallen

With proud thanksgiving, a mother for her children,
    England mourns for her dead across the sea.
Flesh of her flesh they were, spirit of her spirit,
    Fallen in the cause of the free.

Solemn the drums thrill: Death august and royal
    Sings sorrow up into immortal spheres.
There is music in the midst of desolation
    And a glory that shines upon our tears.

They went with songs to the battle, they were young,
    Straight of limb, true of eye, steady and aglow.
They were staunch to the end against odds uncounted,
    They fell with their faces to the foe.

They shall grow not old, as we that are left grow old;
    Age shall not weary them, nor the years condemn.
At the going down of the sun and in the morning
    We will remember them.

They mingle not with their laughing comrades again;
  They sit no more at familiar tables at home;
They have no lot in our labour of the day-time;
  They sleep beyond England's foam.

But where our desires are and our hopes profound,
  Felt as a well-spring that is hidden from sight,
To the innermost heart of their own land they are known
  As the stars are known to the Night;

As the stars that shall be bright when we are dust,
  Moving in marches upon the heavenly plain,
As the stars that are starry in the time of our darkness,
  To the end, to the end, they remain.

Laurence Binyon

In the Trenches

I snatched two poppies
  From the parapet's ledge,
Two bright red poppies
  That winked on the ledge.
Behind my ear
  I stuck one through,
One blood red poppy
  I gave to you.

The sandbags narrowed
  And screwed out our jest,
And tore the poppy
  You had on your breast . . .
Down – a shell – O! Christ,
  I am choked . . . safe . . . dust blind, I
See trench floor poppies
  Strewn. Smashed you lie.

Isaac Rosenberg

August 1914

What in our lives is burnt
   In the fire of this?
The heart's dear granary?
  The much we shall miss?

Three lives hath one life –
   Iron, honey, gold.
The gold, the honey gone –
   Left is the hard and cold.

Iron are our lives
   Molten right through our youth.
A burnt space through ripe fields
   A fair mouth's broken tooth.

Isaac Rosenberg

Dulce et Decorum Est

Bent double, like old beggars under sacks,
    Knock-kneed, coughing like hags, we cursed through sludge,
Till on the haunting flares we turned our backs
    And towards our distant rest began to trudge.
Men marched asleep. Many had lost their boots
    But limped on, blood-shod. All went lame; all blind;
Drunk with fatigue; deaf even to the hoots
    Of tired, outstripped Five-Nines that dropped behind.

Gas! GAS! Quick, boys! – An ecstasy of fumbling,
    Fitting the clumsy helmets just in time;
But someone still was yelling out and stumbling
    And flound'ring like a man in fire or lime . . .
Dim, through the misty panes and thick green light,
    As under I green sea, I saw him drowning.

In all my dreams, before my helpless sight,
He plunges at me, guttering, choking, drowning.

Wilfred Owen

Glory of Women

You love us when we're heroes, home on leave,
   Or wounded in a mentionable place.
You worship decorations; you believe
   That chivalry redeems the war's disgrace.
You make us shells. You listen with delight,
   By tales of dirt and danger fondly thrilled.
You crown our distant ardours while we fight,
   And mourn our laurelled memories when we're killed.
You can't believe that British troops 'retire'
   When hell's last horror breaks them, and they run,
Trampling the terrible corpses-blind with blood.
   O German mother dreaming by the fire,
While you are knitting socks to send your son
   His face is trodden deeper in the mud.

Siegfried Sassoon

When You See Millions of the Mouthless Dead

When you see millions of the mouthless dead
　　Across your dreams in pale battalions go,
Say not soft things as other men have said,
　　That you'll remember. For you need not so.
Give them not praise. For, deaf, how should they know
　　It is not curses heaped on each gashed head?
Nor tears. Their blind eyes see not your tears flow.
　　Nor honour. It is easy to be dead.
Say only this, 'They are dead.' Then add thereto,
　　'Yet many a better one has died before.'
Then, scanning all the o'ercrowded mass, should you
　　Perceive one face that you loved heretofore,
It is a spook. None wears the face you knew.
Great death has made all his for evermore.

Charles Hamilton Sorley

To Germany

You are blind like us. Your hurt no man designed,
    And no man claimed the conquest of your land.
But gropers both through fields of thought confined
    We stumble and we do not understand.
You only saw your future bigly planned,
    And we, the tapering paths of our own mind,
And in each other's dearest ways we stand,
    And hiss and hate. And the blind fight the blind.

When it is peace, then we may view again
    With new-won eyes each other's truer form
And wonder. Grown more loving-kind and warm
    We'll grasp firm hands and laugh at the old pain,
When it is peace. But until peace, the storm
    The darkness and the thunder and the rain.

Charles Hamilton Sorley

England to Germany in 1914

'O England, may God punish thee!'
– Is it that Teuton genius flowers
Only to breathe malignity
Upon its friend of earlier hours?
– We have eaten your bread, you have eaten ours,
We have loved your burgs, your pines' green moan,
Fair Rhine-stream, and its storied towers;
Your shining souls of deathless dowers
Have won us as they were our own:

We have nursed no dreams to shed your blood,
We have matched your might not rancorously,
Save a flushed few whose blatant mood
You heard and marked as well as we
To tongue not in their country's key;
But yet you cry with face aflame,
'O England, may God punish thee!'
And foul in onward history,
And present sight, your ancient name.

Thomas Hardy

The Pity Of It

I walked in loamy Wessex lanes, afar
From rail-track and from highway, and I heard
In field and farmstead many an ancient word
Of local lineage like 'Thu bist,' 'Er war,'
'Ich woll,' 'Er sholl,' and by-talk similar,
Nigh as they speak who in this month's moon gird
At England's very loins, thereunto spurred
By gangs whose glory threats and slaughters are.

Then seemed a Heart crying: 'Whosoever they be
At root and bottom of this, who flung this flame
Between kin folk kin tongued even as are we,
Sinister, ugly, lurid, be their fame;
May their familiars grow to shun their name,
And their brood perish everlastingly.'

Thomas Hardy

Two Sonnets

I

Saints have adored the lofty soul of you.
Poets have whitened at your high renown.
We stand among the many millions who
Do hourly wait to pass your pathway down.

You, so familiar, once were strange: we tried
To live as of your presence unaware.
But now in every road on every side
We see your straight and steadfast signpost there.

I think it like that signpost in my land
Hoary and tall, which pointed me to go
Upward, into the hills, on the right hand,
Where the mists swim and the winds shriek and blow,
A homeless land and friendless, but a land
I did not know and that I wished to know.

II

Such, such is Death: no triumph: no defeat:
Only an empty pail, a slate rubbed clean,
A merciful putting away of what has been.

And this we know: Death is not Life effete,
Life crushed, the broken pail. We who have seen
So marvellous things know well the end not yet.

Victor and vanquished are a-one in death:
Coward and brave: friend, foe. Ghosts do not say,
'Come, what was your record when you drew breath?'
But a big blot has hid each yesterday
So poor, so manifestly incomplete.
And your bright Promise, withered long and sped,
Is touched; stirs, rises, opens and grows sweet
And blossoms and is you, when you are dead.

Charles Hamilton Sorley

Break of Day in the Trenches

The darkness crumbles away
   It is the same old druid Time as ever,
Only a live thing leaps my hand,
   A queer sardonic rat,
As I pull the parapet's poppy
   To stick behind my ear.
Droll rat, they would shoot you if they knew
   Your cosmopolitan sympathies,
Now you have touched this English hand
   You will do the same to a German
Soon, no doubt, if it be your pleasure
   To cross the sleeping green between.
It seems you inwardly grin as you pass
   Strong eyes, fine limbs, haughty athletes,
Less chanced than you for life,
   Bonds to the whims of murder,
Sprawled in the bowels of the earth,
   The torn fields of France.

What do you see in our eyes
    At the shrieking iron and flame
Hurled through still heavens?
    What quaver – what heart aghast?
Poppies whose roots are in men's veins
    Drop, and are ever dropping;
But mine in my ear is safe,
    Just a little white with the dust.

Isaac Rosenberg

WORLD WAR II

Origins of World War II

After the horrors of World War I, the major powers were not satisfied with the outcome and felt that the Treaty of Versailles was not appeasing the situation. On the one hand, Germany bitterly resented the losses of territory and the enforced payment for reparations imposed on it by the treaty. Germany felt they had been treated badly and wanted revenge. Italy, one of the victors in the conflict, was also far from happy about its territorial gains, when compared to its losses during the war. Japan, too, was unhappy about its failure to gain control of China.

On the other hand, France, Great Britain and the United States believed that they had achieved their wartime objectives. They had reduced the military power of Germany and also felt they had reorganised Europe as they saw fit. Keen to keep a stable level of peace, they formed the League of Nations in 1920. It was designed as a forum in which nation's could air their dissatisfaction and try to settle their disputes. However, the League of Nations was weak right from the start. Having failed to achieve disarmament and after spectacular failures in both Manchuria and Abyssinia, disillusioned countries starting to resign from the League, realising that they would have to fight a war to settle their differences.

The peace-making terms of the Treaty of Versailles, rather than offer appeasement to troubled nations, seemed to encourage war. Feeling that he had been pushed too far, Hitler was ready to fight. Many historians feel that the World War II was Hitler's own personal war and that he always intended to fight in an effort to save face after the disasters of World War I.

All this anger among the nations grew, until Chamberlain declared war on Hitler on 3 September 1939. In terms of lives lost and material destruction, World War II was the most devastating conflict in the history of mankind. It started as a European conflict between Germany and an Anglo-French coalition, but ended up involving the rest of the world. It killed more people, cost more money, damaged more property and caused more far-reaching changes in nearly every country than any other war. The number of people killed throughout the war can only be estimated, but it is believed that as many as 55 million lives were lost. More than 50 countries took part and there wasn't one corner of our continent that did not feel its effects.

So how did the various countries feel the effects of World War II?

Germany was totally defeated and the Nazi regime crumbled. Its leaders were eventually tried for crimes against humanity, but Hitler himself escaped the trial by committing suicide in his Berlin bunker at the end of the war.

Like Germany, Japan was also in ruins following extensive bombing campaigns. Prominent Japanese military leaders were tried and convicted of war crimes, but the emperor was allowed to retain his position.

Britain, having experienced extensive bombing during the 1940 blitz by the Germans, had the massive task of rebuilding many of its cities. The British had to seek economic aid from other countries and eventually phased out the remainder of its imperial holdings.

France, who had not experienced enormous losses in World War I, had to recover from the effects of Nazi occupation during World War II. France was compelled to dismantle its colonial empire, but first fought long and bitter wars in an effort to maintain control.

Although Russia had suffered immeasurably during the war, they did manage to build a large and powerful army which occupied the majority of Eastern Europe by the end of the conflict. With these resources and the size of their population, Russia was a main contender, along with the United States, to become one of the new superpowers.

The United States was the country who came out on top at the end of the war, with less destruction and their economy still intact. After four years of building up a strong military power, they were left in the position of being a major world leader.

⤶⤷

When we think about war poets, the poets of World War I immediately spring to mind. Their powerful experiences of life in the horrific trenches of the Somme and elsewhere were reflected in their poetry, but sadly such luminaries as Wilfred Owen, Isaac Rosenberg, Rupert Brooke and Edward Thomas all lost their lives fighting for their country. By comparison, the number of poets who wrote about World War II is relatively few. The three poets who do represent this period are Sidney Keyes, Keith Douglas and Alun Lewis, all of whom were soldiers in active service. Dylan Thomas, on the other hand, found the idea of war completely ridiculous and stated quite categorically that he would not be able to kill another human being. He did everything in his power not to drafted into the army, but used his time writing scripts for wartime documentaries. One of his poems, 'A Refusal to Mourn the Death, by Fire, of a Child in London', portrayed his sentiments about the futility of war.

At A War Grave

No grave is rich, the dust that herein lies
    Beneath this white cross mixing with the sand
Was vital once, with skill of eye and hand
    And speed of brain. These will not re-arise
These riches, nor will they be replaced;
    They are lost and nothing now, and here is left
Only a worthless corpse of sense bereft,
    Symbol of death, and sacrifice and waste.

John Jarmain

A Refusal to Mourn the Death, by Fire, of a Child in London

Never until the mankind making
   Bird, beast and flower
Fathering and all humbling darkness
   Tells with silence the last light breaking
And the still hour
   Is come of the sea tumbling in harness

And I must enter again the round
   Zion of the water bead
And the synagogue of the ear of corn
   Shall I let pray the shadow of a sound
Or sow my salt seed
   In the least valley of sackcloth to mourn

The majesty and burning of the child's death.
   I shall not murder
The mankind of her going with a grave truth
   Nor blaspheme down the stations of the breath
With any further
   Elegy of innocence and youth.

Deep with the first dead lies London's daughter,
   Robed in the long friends,
The grains beyond age, the dark veins of her mother,
   Secret by the unmourning water
Of the riding Thames.
   After the first death, there is no other.

Dylan Thomas

Actors Waiting in the Wings of Europe

Actors waiting in the wings of Europe
    we already watch the lights on the stage
and listen to the colossal overture begin.
    For us entering at the height of the din
it will be hard to hear our thoughts, hard to gauge
    how much our conduct owes to fear or fury.

Everyone, I suppose, will use these minutes
    to look back, to hear music and recall
what we were doing and saying that year
    during our last few months as people, near
the sucking mouth of the day that swallowed us all
    into the stomach of a war. Now we are in it

and no more people, just little pieces of food
    swirling in an uncomfortable digestive journey,
what we said and did then has a slightly
    fairytale quality. There is an excitement
in seeing our ghosts wandering

(The final stanza of this poem is incomplete.)

Keith Douglas

All Day It Has Rained

All day it has rained, and we on the edge of the moors
Have sprawled in our bell-tents, moody and dull as boors,
Groundsheets and blankets spread on the muddy ground
And from the first grey wakening we have found
No refuge from the skirmishing fine rain
And the wind that made the canvas heave and flap
And the taut wet guy-ropes ravel out and snap.
All day the rain has glided, wave and mist and dream,
Drenching the gorse and heather, a gossamer stream
Too light to stir the acorns that suddenly
Snatched from their cups by the wild south-westerly
Pattered against the tent and our upturned dreaming faces.
And we stretched out, unbuttoning our braces,
Smoking a Woodbine, darning dirty socks,
Reading the Sunday papers – I saw a fox
And mentioned it in the note I scribbled home; –
And we talked of girls and dropping bombs on Rome,

And thought of the quiet dead and the loud celebrities
Exhorting us to slaughter, and the herded refugees;

As of ourselves or those whom we
For years have loved, and will again
Tomorrow maybe love; but now it is the rain
Possesses us entirely, the twilight and the rain.

And I can remember nothing dearer or more to my heart
Than the children I watched in the woods on Saturday
Shaking down burning chestnuts for the schoolyard's merry play,
Or the shaggy patient dog who followed me
By Sheet and Steep and up the wooded scree
To the Shoulder o' Mutton where Edward Thomas brooded long
On death and beauty – till a bullet stopped his song.

Alun Lewis

Aristocrats

'I Think I Am Becoming A God'

The noble horse with courage in his eye,
 clean in the bone, looks up at a shellburst:
away fly the images of the shires
 but he puts the pipe back in his mouth.
Peter was unfortunately killed by an 88;
 it took his leg away, he died in the ambulance.
I saw him crawling on the sand, he said
 It's most unfair, they've shot my foot off.

How can I live among this gentle
 obsolescent breed of heroes, and not weep?
Unicorns, almost,
 for they are fading into two legends
in which their stupidity and chivalry
 are celebrated. Each, fool and hero, will be an immortal.

These plains were their cricket pitch
     and in the mountains the tremendous drop fences
brought down some of the runners. Here then
     under the stones and earth they dispose themselves,
I think with their famous unconcern.
     It is not gunfire I hear, but a hunting horn.

Keith Douglas

Beach Burial

Softly and humbly to the Gulf of Arabs
    The convoys of dead sailors come;
At night they sway and wander in the waters far under,
    But morning rolls them in the foam.

Between the sob and clubbing of gunfire
    Someone, it seems, has time for this,
To pluck them from the shallows and bury them in burrows
    And tread the sand upon their nakedness;

And each cross, the driven stake of tidewood,
    Bears the last signature of men,
Written with such perplexity, with such bewildered pity,
    The words choke as they begin -

'Unknown seaman' – the ghostly pencil
    Wavers and fades, the purple drips,
The breath of wet season has washed their inscriptions
    As blue as drowned men's lips,

Dead seamen, gone in search of the same landfall,
    Whether as ememies they fought,
Or fought with us, or neither; the sand joins them together,
    Enlisted on the other front.

Kenneth Slessor

Can You Take It?

This poem was found written on the wall of a solitary confinement cell at Dulag Luft. Nearly all captured Allied airmen were sent there to be interrogated before being assigned to a permanent prison camp.

It's easy to be nice, boys
　When everything's O.K.
It's easy to be cheerful,
　When your having things your way.
But can you hold your head up
　And take it on the chin.
When your heart is breaking
　And you feel like giving in?

It was easy back in England,
　Among the friends and folks.
But now you miss the friendly hand,
　The joys, and songs, and jokes.
The road ahead is stormy.
　And unless you're strong in mind,

You'll find it isn't long before
  You're dragging far behind.

You've got to climb the hill, boys;
  It's no use turning back.
There's only one way home, boys,
  And it's off the beaten track.
Remember you're American,
  And when you reach the crest,
You'll see a valley cool and green,
  Our country at its best.

You know there is a saying
  That sunshine follows rain,
And sure enough you'll realize
  That joy will follow pain.
Let courage be your password,
  Make fortitude your guide;
And then instead of grousing,
  Just remember those who died.

Anonymous

Desert Flowers

Living in a wide landscape are the flowers –
Rosenberg I only repeat what you were saying –
the shell and the hawk every hour
are slaying men and jerboas, slaying
the mind: but the body can fill
the hungry flowers and the dogs who cry words
at nights, the most hostile things of all.
But that is not new. Each time the night discards
draperies on the eyes and leaves the mind awake
I look each side of the door of sleep
for the little coin it will take
to buy the secret I shall not keep.
I see men as trees suffering
or confound the detail and the horizon.
Lay the coin on my tongue and I will sing
of what the others never set eyes on.

Keith Douglas

For Johnny

Do not despair
   For Johnny-head-in-air;
He sleeps as sound
   As Johnny underground.

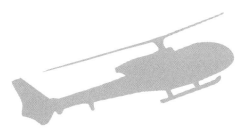

Fetch out no shroud
   For Johnny-in-the-cloud;
And keep your tears
   For him in after years.

Better by far
   For Johnny-the-bright-star,
To keep your head,
   And see his children fed.

John Pudney

A Combat Airman's Prayer

Please dear God, just let me soar
O'er green and yellow fields, once more
Where there'll be on dirty clouds of black
Bringing forth the anguished cry of 'flak'.

Where sight of a speck out in the blue,
Will not mean 'watch it – fighter or two'
As out of the sun streaks a blazing Hun
To make every man jump, and with a blazing gun.

Endeavour to pay another life
To the devil who started this world strife
If you don't think this too much a boon,
Please dear God, please make it soon.

Anonymous

Raiders' Dawn

Softly the civilized
    Centuries fall,
Paper on paper,
    Peter on Paul.

And lovers walking
    From the night –
Eternity's masters,
    Slaves of Time –
Recognize only
    The drifting white
Fall of small faces
    In pits of lime.

Blue necklace left
    On a charred chair
Tells that Beauty
    Was startled there.

Alun Lewis

How To Kill

Under the parabola of a ball,
   a child turning into a man,
I looked into the air too long.
   The ball fell in my hand, it sang
in the closed fist: Open Open
   Behold a gift designed to kill.

Now in my dial of glass appears
   the soldier who is going to die.
He smiles, and moves about in ways
   his mother knows, habits of his.
The wires touch his face: I cry
   NOW. Death, like a familiar, hears

and look, has made a man of dust
    of a man of flesh. This sorcery
I do. Being damned, I am amused
    to see the centre of love diffused
and the wave of love travel into vacancy.
    How easy it is to make a ghost.

The weightless mosquito touches
    her tiny shadow on the stone,
and with how like, how infinite
    a lightness, man and shadow meet.
They fuse. A shadow is a man
    when the mosquito death approaches.

Keith Douglas

Simplify Me When I'm Dead

Remember me when I am dead
and simplify me when I'm dead.

As the processes of earth
strip off the colour of the skin:
take the brown hair and blue eye

and leave me simpler than at birth,
when hairless I came howling in
as the moon entered the cold sky.

Of my skeleton perhaps,
so stripped, a learned man will say
'He was of such a type and intelligence', no more.

Thus when in a year collapse
particular memories, you may
deduce, from the long pain I bore

the opinions I held, who was my foe
and what I left, even my appearance
but incidents will be no guide.

Time's wrong-way telescope will show
a minute man ten years hence
and by distance simplified.

Through that lens see if I seem
substance or nothing: of the world
deserving mention or charitable oblivion,

not by momentary spleen
or love into decision hurled,
leisurely arrive at an opinion.

Remember me when I am dead
and simplify me when I'm dead.

Keith Douglas

Vergissmeinnicht ('Forget-me-not')

Elegy for an 88 Gunner

Three weeks gone and the combatants gone
returning over the nightmare ground
we found the place again, and found
the soldier sprawling in the sun.

The frowning barrel of his gun
overshadowing. As we came on
that day, he hit my tank with one
like the entry of a demon.

Look. Here in the gunpit spoil
the dishonoured picture of his girl
who has put: Steffi. Vergissmeinnicht
in a copybook gothic script.

We see him almost with content,
abased, and seeming to have paid
and mocked at by his own equipment
that's hard and good when he's decayed.

But she would weep to see today
how on his skin the swart flies move;
the dust upon the paper eye
and the burst stomach like a cave.

For here the lover and killer are mingled
who had one body and one heart.
And death who had the soldier singled
has done the lover mortal hurt.

Keith Douglas

Landscape: Western Desert

Winds carve this land
And velvet whorls of sand
Annul footprint and grave
Of lover, fool and knave.
Briefly the vetches bloom
In the blind desert room
When humble, bright and brave
Met common doom.

Their gear and shift
Smother in soft sand-drift,
Less perishable, less
Soon in rottenness.
Their war-spent tools of trade
In the huge space parade;
And with this last distress,
All scores are paid.

And who will see,
In such last anarchy
Of loveless lapse and loss
Which the blind sands now gloss,
the common heart which meant
Such good in its intent;
Such noble common dross
Suddenly spent.

John Pudney

An Inscription for Dog River

Our general was the greatest and bravest of generals.
For his deeds, look around you on this coast –
Here is his name cut next to Ashur-Bani-Pal's,
Nebuchadnezzar's and the Roman host;
And we, though our identities have been lost,
Lacking the validity of stone or metal,
We, too, are part of his memorial,
Having been put in for the cost,
Having bestowed on him all we had to give
In battles few can recollect,
Our strength, obedience and endurance,
Our wits, our bodies, our existence,
Even our descendants' right to live –
Having given him everything, in fact,
Except respect.

Kenneth Slessor

Combat Report

'Just then I saw the bloody Hun'
You saw the Hun? You, light and easy,
Carving the soundless daylight. 'I was breezy
When I saw that Hun.' Oh wonder
Pattern of stress, of nerve poise, flyer,
Overtaking time. 'He came out under
Nine-tenths cloud, but I was higher.'
Did Michelangelo aspire,
Painting the laughing cimulus, to ride
The majesty of air. 'He was a trier
I'll give him that, the Hun.' So you covert
Ultimate sky of air speed, drift and cover;
Sure with the tricky tools of God and lover.
'I let him have a sharp four-second squirt,
Closing to fifty yards. He went on fire.'
Your deadly petals painted, you exert
A simple stature. Man-high, without pride,
You pick your way through heaven and the dirt.
'He burnt out in the air; that's how the poor sod died.'

John Pudney

THE
VIETNAM
WAR

Origins of the Vietnam War

For the majority of Vietnam's history, it has been under foreign rule. France's domination began in 1860 and by the end of the 19th century it had accomplished colonisation in a number of regions around the Gulf of Tonkin. When World War II broke out, the Japanese played their part and took control of a large area, setting up a puppet regime. This stayed in place until the end of the war when the Vietnamese forced them out.

From the end of World War II right up until 1955, France strived to regain its former territories. However, with a weak and diminished army who had no desire to fight, their efforts were in vain. The French were finally defeated at Dien Bien Phy on 8 May 1954, forcing them to withdraw. This left the area free and the North and South set up elections. The Communists set up their headquarters in Hanoi under the leadership of Ho Chi Minh. Those Vietnamese who didn't want the oppression of a communist regime, fled south where Ngo Dinh Diem had formed the Republic of Vietnam.

Between 1955 and 1960, the north and the south of the country were in bitter conflict. In November 1963 President Diem was executed, and the North Vietnamese began a massive move to take over the whole country – aided by the powerful nations of China and Russia. Fearing that the Communists would conquer the entire territory, the United States became increasingly worried.

Although the United States wanted to stop the spread of Communism, they knew that if they became involved this could create tensions with the Chinese and Russians which, they feared, could lead to World War III. However, with the Vietnamese army in disarray and suffering from low morale, the United States felt it had had no other option than to send in troops. Although they initially were sent in to take an advisory role, the conflict soon escalated into a full blown war.

The US President, Lyndon B. Johnson replaced John F. Kennedy following his assassination in 1963. Johnson was too worried about his own image to halt the escalating war in Vietnam and, despite actually having the power to do so, he didn't want to be regarded as the first US president to actually lose a war. Soon the pressure was so great for him to do something about the war that he decided not to run for a second term, and left the problem to his predecessor, Richard M. Nixon.

LIFE IN THE JUNGLE

The US commander in Vietnam was General William Westmoreland, and he had the problem of how to cope with immature soldiers in an environment which was totally alien to them. Added to that, the enemy, who were used to the jungle conditions, could hide anywhere and take the US soldiers by surprise. To try and survive the harsh living conditions, many of the soldiers resorted to taking drugs and other stimulants and morale quickly declined. Back at home riots and demonstrations against the war in Vietnam became a regular occurrence. Finally, the US government realised they were in a no-win situation and began making plans to withdraw their troops.

After establishing a ceasefire on 27 January 1973, the US were eventually able to start pulling their soldiers out of Vietnam for good. The North Vietnamese went on to conquer the South, totally ignoring the ceasefire. On 2 July 1976, exactly as the US feared, the North and South of Vietnam were officially united as a single Communist state.

The most immediate effect of the Vietnam War was the staggering number of deaths. The war is estimated to have killed as many as two million Vietnamese civilians, 1.1 million North Vietnamese soldiers, 200,000 South Vietnamese soldiers and 58,000 US troops. The wounded were estimated in tens of thousands. The massive bombing raids by the US Army left Vietnam in ruins and the use of herbicides not only devastated the country's natural environment but caused widespread health problems that have persisted for decades.

The subject of the Vietnam War continues to raise issues decades later. Even though it was small in terms of geographical area when compared to the two great world wars, it still had a devastating effect.

❧ ✿ ☙

The poems in this section are both moving and shocking and bring home to the reader the conditions that soldiers on both sides had to contend with. Many were little more than children. These words come from the pens of those affected by the cruelty and harshness of war.

America – 'My Country 'tis of Thee'

Here I sit in shit and mud
And wipe the dried and caking blood
From my dead friends face. The littered zone
Is full of young men going home
In dirty ponchos. Their lives so fast undone
As from their lips, forever dumb
They scream in silent shock and fear
In frozen agony. Quietly, they lie so near
In sleeping rank and file. Who might know
What thought flashed at the jolting blow
That ripped the jagged hole? What sound
Escaped them as they pitched to ground
To bubble out their scarlet life? What tears,
Welled up to grasp those unsaid fears
Had at last come true! No tears now,
Just swarming flies fill their vacant, sightless eyes.

Curt Bennett
(Former US pilot on active service in Vietnam)

The Green Beret

This poem was found on Ho Thien's dead body sometime in 1966 near the Cambodian border.

He was twelve years old,
   and I do not know his name.
The mercenaries took him and his father,
   whose name I do not know,
one morning upon the High Plateau.
Green beret looked down on the frail boy
   with the eyes of a hurt animal and thought,
a good fright will make him talk.
   He commanded, and the father was taken away
behind the forest's green wall.
   'Right kid tell us where they are,
tell us where or your father – dead.'
   With eyes now bright and filled with terror
the slight boy said nothing.
   'You've got one minute kid,' said Green Beret,
'tell us where or we kill father'
   and thrust his wrist-watch against a face all eyes,
the second-hand turning, jerking on its way.
   'OK boy ten seconds to tell us where they are'
In the last instant the silver hand shattered the
   sky and the forest of trees.

'Kill the old guy' roared Green Beret
    and shots hammered out
behind the forest's green wall
    and sky and trees and soldiers stood
in silence, and the boy cried out.
    Green Beret stood
in silence, as the boy crouched down
    and shook with tears,
as children do when their father dies.
    Christ, said one mercenary to Green beret,
'He didn't know a damn thing
    we killed the old guy for nothing.'
So they all went away,
    green beret and his mercenaries.

And the boy knew everything.
    He knew everything about them, the caves,
the trails, the hidden places and the names,
    and in the moment that he cried out,
in that same instant,
    protected by frail tears
far stronger than any wall of steel,
    they passed everywhere
like tigers
    across the High Plateau.

Song of the Hammock

The hammock chirps, the hammock sings,
My hand rocks to its cadence.
The three rooms of my straw hut
Fill with the hammock's song.

The hammock chirps, the hammock sings,
The summer noon spreads everywhere.
Settled on a single foot,
A bird nods drowsing on bamboo.

The hammock chirps, the hammock sings,
The custard apple tree sleeps:
Its fruit looks through half-open eyes,
The sky burning blue.

The hammock chirps, the hammock sings,
The hammock softly sways.
There at the open window
A bird taps out a rhythm.

The hammock chirps, the hammock sings
How many years rocked by my mother

To the same hammock's sound?
Far away the white egret flies.

The hammock chirps, the hammock sings,
Little Giang already sleeps,
Her hair moving to its sway,
Her lips sketched into a smile.

In her dreams
She runs by the edge of the river
Chasing a white stork,
A giant gold butterfly.

She sees our mother
Bending over in the rice field,
Sees the gunners on the watch
Guarding our blue sky.

Rockaby, my little sister
My hand rocks in cadence.
Rockaby, my little sister.

Tran Dang Khoa
(Translated by Nguyen Khac Viens)

Vietnamese Morning

Before war starts
   In early morning
The land is breath taking.
   The low, blazing, ruby sun
Melts the night-shadow pools
   Creating an ethereal appearance.

Each miniature house and tree
   Sprouts its, long, thin shadow
Stretching long on dewy ground.
   The countryside is panoramic maze,
Jungle, hamlets, hills and waterways,
   Bomb-craters, paddies, broken-backed bridges.

Rice fields glow sky-sheens,
   Flat, calm, mirrored lakes
Reflect the morning peace.
   The patchwork quilted earth,
Slashed by snaking tree-lines,
   Slumbers in dawn's blue light.

Sharp, rugged mountain peaks
   Sleep in a soft rolling blanket
Of clinging, slippery, misty fog.
   Effortlessly, languidly, it flows
Shyly spreading wispy tentacles out
   To embrace the earth with velvet arms.

Curt Bennett

He Was A Mate

He was a mate, a real good mate 'e was,
    A friendly sort of feller, liked a joke;
And if it had to happen, it's a shame
    It had to happen to such a decent bloke.

But – ah, fair dinkum, don't it make you wonder
    What God in Heaven's thinkin' about up there;
The way He chooses who to sacrifice
    To me somehow it doesn't quite seem fair.

You'd think He'd want to take a bloke like me
    Who'd be no loss to no-one here on Earth;
But no, He always seems to pick the best
    Whose life amounts to ten times what mine's worth.

But I suppose He'd say it's not His fault,
    It's us and how we treat our fellow man;
And if too many good blokes' lives are lost
    We can't just blame it all on His great plan.

He slung us here on Earth and said 'Righto,
    Get on with it you blokes, the world is yours';
But all we've done is fight among ourselves
    And destroy each other with our endless wars.

Now, there's a sort of aching here inside,
    I can't quite put my finger on what's wrong;
But a soldier can't afford to feel this way,
    He's got to grit his teeth and carry on.

So how's a bloke supposed to deal with this?
    I know they trained me well, I can't complain;
But this is somethin' you don't learn about
    When they teach you how to play the soldier's game.

They teach you how to shoot and how to kill,
    You even learn which enemy to hate;
But nowhere in their training do you learn
    How to live with the loss of a real good mate.

Lachlan Irvine
(Australian Vietnam Forces)

The Wounded and the Dead

I was just a child,
   When they sent me to Vietnam,
The fateful day I landed there,
   Reality hit me like a bomb.
I saw the remains of a human being,
   Like a pile of rags in the street,
And innocent children blown away,
   With mines beneath their feet.
I still remember the poor soldier,
   That in the confusion lost his mind,
Only then to lose his life,
   As he was left behind.
I saw the wounded and the dead,
   Trying to identify boys that had no face,
I heard comrades cry for their mothers,
   Don't let me die in this foreign place.
With a fear that's all consuming,
   Looking for a place to hide,
I saw men pulling down on their helmets,
   And try curling up inside.

When surrounded by the enemy,
  I called in artillery over my own head,
In the morning there was nothing left,
  As I alone walked through the dead.
Fighting for an unknown cause,
  I still can't understand why,
In the jungles of Vietnam,
  So many soldiers had to die.
All those images still haunt me,
  As if it were yesterday,
Remembering all those brave young men,
  And the price they had to pay.
I've seen the wounded and the dead,
  And though our country's free,
I remain a prisoner of war,
  Being tortured by its memory.

Chris Woolnough

The Nightmare Never Ends

Close your eyes and go to sleep,
  My poor, haunted soldier man,
I'll try my best to keep you safe,
  In any way I possibly can.

Cradled there in my loving arms,
  He drifted off to Vietnam once more.
I tried my best to soothe him,
  But he was already back in the war.

His body's tense and twitching,
  As he dreams of yesteryear,
I call out his name in vane,
  Just trying to ease his fear.

But the battle is already brewing,
  He's in the mist of a fire fight,
And for what seems like an eternity,
  My soldier thrashes in the night.

And it's too late to bring him home,
   He's fighting alongside his brothers,
He hears his comrades cry out in pain,
   And call out for their mothers.

He's soaked in sweat as he jumps about,
   He feels the bullets whizzing by,
His body's numb as he checks himself,
   He's so certain he's gonna die.

No, not today my brave hero,
   Though you've lost so many friends,
He opens his eyes as the dream has past,
   But the nightmare never ends.

Chris Woolnough

WAR
CLASSICS

Once more unto the breach, dear friends, once more . . .

These famous words come from the 'Cry God for Harry, England, and Saint George!' speech in William Shakespeare's *Henry V*, Act III, written in 1599. The word 'breach' refers to a gap in the wall of the city of Hafleur which was being held under siege by the English army. These words were intended as encouragement by the king for his troops to muster the strenth to attack the city again.

> Once more unto the breach, dear friends, once more;
> Or close the wall up with our English dead.
> In peace there's nothing so becomes a man
> As modest stillness and humility:
> But when the blast of war blows in our ears,
> Then imitate the action of the tiger;
> Stiffen the sinews, summon up the blood,
> Disguise fair nature with hard-favour'd rage;
> Then lend the eye a terrible aspect;
> Let pry through the portage of the head
> Like the brass cannon; let the brow o'erwhelm it
> As fearfully as doth a galled rock

O'erhang and jutty his confounded base,
Swill'd with the wild and wasteful ocean.
Now set the teeth and stretch the nostril wide,
Hold hard the breath and bend up every spirit
To his full height. On, on, you noblest English.
Whose blood is fet from fathers of war-proof!
Fathers that, like so many Alexanders,
Have in these parts from morn till even fought
And sheathed their swords for lack of argument:
Dishonour not your mothers; now attest
That those whom you call'd fathers did beget you.
Be copy now to men of grosser blood,
And teach them how to war. And you, good yeoman,
Whose limbs were made in England, show us here
The mettle of your pasture; let us swear
That you are worth your breeding; which I doubt not;
For there is none of you so mean and base,
That hath not noble lustre in your eyes.
I see you stand like greyhounds in the slips,
Straining upon the start. The game's afoot:
Follow your spirit, and upon this charge
Cry 'God for Harry, England, and Saint George!'

William Shakespeare

The Charge of the Light Brigade

The 'Charge of the Light Brigade' by Alfred Tennyson was written in 1864 and commemorates a rather non-descript incident which took place during the Crimean War. The Light Brigade — cavalry bearing only light arms — were attempting to capture the Russian gun redoubts at Balaclava, but the whole manouvre went terribly wrong. Of the 673 men who charged down 'The Valley of Death', only 195 survived. When news of the debacle reached London, there was a public outcry.

> Half a league, half a league,
> Half a league onward,
> All in the valley of Death
> Rode the six hundred.
> 'Forward, the Light Brigade!'
> 'Charge for the guns!' he said:
> Into the valley of Death
> Rode the six hundred.
>
> 'Forward, the Light Brigade!'
> Was there a man dismay'd?
> Not tho' the soldier knew
> Someone had blunder'd:
> Their's not to make reply,

Their's not to reason why,
Their's but to do and die:
Into the valley of Death
Rode the six hundred.

Cannon to right of them,
Cannon to left of them,
Cannon in front of them
Volley'd and thunder'd;
Storm'd at with shot and shell,
Boldly they rode and well,
Into the jaws of Death,
Into the mouth of Hell
Rode the six hundred.
Flash'd all their sabres bare,
Flash'd as they turn'd in air,
Sabring the gunners there,
Charging an army, while
All the world wonder'd:
Plunged in the battery-smoke
Right thro' the line they broke;
Cossack and Russian
Reel'd from the sabre stroke
Shatter'd and sunder'd.

Then they rode back, but not
Not the six hundred.

Cannon to right of them,
Cannon to left of them,
Cannon behind them
Volley'd and thunder'd;
Storm'd at with shot and shell,
While horse and hero fell,
They that had fought so well
Came thro' the jaws of Death
Back from the mouth of Hell,
All that was left of them,
Left of six hundred.

When can their glory fade?
O the wild charge they made!
All the world wondered.
Honor the charge they made,
Honor the Light Brigade,
Noble six hundred.

Alfred, Lord Tennyson

Index